NOSTRADAMUS AND VISIONS OF THE FUTURE

Abbeydale Press

Published by Abbeydale Press
an imprint of Bookmart Ltd
Registered Number 2372865
Trading as Bookmart Ltd, Desford Road, Enderby
Leicester LE9 5AD

Printed in the Slovak Republic
50978/3

ISBN 1-86147-013-4

Every effort has been made to contact the copyright holders for the pictures.
In some cases they have been untraceable, for which we offer our apologies.
Thanks to the Hulton Deutsch Collection Ltd, who supplied most of them.
Pictures have been provided as follows: Island Publishing Co (pp 75, 76 top),
Popperfoto (p 72) and *Psychic News* (pp 68 bottom, 78).
The remainder have been supplied by the Hulton Deutsch Collection Ltd.

The Author
Allan Hall is a professional journalist currently working in
New York as a foreign correspondent. He is the author of
several books on mysteries, scandals and murders.

NOSTRADAMUS AND VISIONS OF THE FUTURE

NOSTRADAMUS –
The Greatest Seer of All

Nearly 500 years ago a medieval doctor retreated to his secret study, night after night, to journey into the future. The images that he saw were so terrifying that he concealed his prophecies in an elaborate code. Now that code has been broken, and history has confirmed the accuracy of many of his predictions – but are the final devastating prophecies about to come true?

History credits a man named Nostradamus as being the greatest seer who ever lived. His prophecies, cast nearly 500 years ago, have been interpreted by learned scholars, laymen and sceptics alike as the first – and accurate – drafts of great world events. Nostradamus correctly foretold the Great Fire of London and the coming of Adolf Hitler. He prophesized the death of Henri II of France, the triumph and death of Elizabeth I of England and the French Revolution. If his last prediction is right – that of a war to end all wars – then civilization as we know it could be destroyed in the year 1999. It is the one prophecy that all students of Nostradamus hope and pray is incorrect – but if his record is anything to go by, mankind should surely fear the worst.

Nostradamus was born Michel de Nostradame in St Remy de Provence on 14 December 1503. His father, James, was a lawyer, born into a Jewish family who had converted to the Catholic faith. Michel was a brilliant student who spent his time in between lessons reading books on fortune telling and the occult. His grandfather, who had a great influence over his schooling, also taught him the 'celestial sciences' – astronomy. After studying

Opposite: Nostradamus, a prophet unsurpassed through the ages whose premonitions foretold of the cataclysmic events which would shape our world. Here the master is pictured in a 1666 engraving which formed the frontispiece of a collection of his prophecies.

The prophet lived in an ordered world where the divine right of kings reigned supreme. What mystical powers, then, did he tap into to foresee the French Revolution and with it the storming of the Bastille (below), where enemies of the state were held in appalling conditions?

> **HIS HAND TREMBLED AS HE WROTE HIS PREDICTIONS: HE WAS RISKING THE TORTURES OF THE HOLY INQUISITION.**

Capricorn, the reaper, pictured (below) *in a medieval German book of astrology. The signs of the planets and their influence upon humankind were of immense interest to Nostradamus.*

humanities at Avignon he went to the University of Montpellier where he read medicine and philosophy. Medicine was to be his first calling and he excelled as a physician. When he was 20 Nostradamus retreated from Montpellier as it was ravaged by the Great Plague laying waste to Europe's cities and villages, but returned two years later, after practising in Bordeaux and Narbonne, to complete his medical degree. It was at this time that he changed his name from Nostradame to Nostradamus, 'Man of Our Lady'.

He left Montpellier for Provence, his home region which was also being decimated by the plague. He soon earned a name for himself as a courageous physician who, regardless of his own safety, began venturing into the worst-stricken areas to aid the sick, but he refused to 'bleed' people, one of the commonest – and cruellest – medical practices of the age. Older and more powerful physicians than Nostradamus expounded the virtues of this nonsensical practice, believing that the illness in an afflicted person's body flowed away with the blood. Instead Nostradamus set about

making compounds and potions to relieve suffering and later noted their compositions in a book.

In 1534 after being invited by a prominent philosopher to stay with him at his home in Agen, Nostradamus met and married a beautiful noblewoman. He had a son and a daughter by her but soon the plague – a virulent strain called '*le charbon*' because sufferers were stricken with great black pustules on their bodies – came to Agen and claimed the lives of his family. Heartbroken, Nostradamus wandered around France for several years; the prime purpose of his travels seems to have been the collection and study of potions and medicines from apothecaries and pharmacists across the land. He also travelled to Italy, where one of the legends about his mystical powers first grew. He saw a young monk leading a herd of swine down a narrow street; as the monk drew level with him Nostradamus bowed down on one knee and addressed him as 'Your Holiness'. Later, the humble swineherd, Felice Peretti, became Pope Sextus V, long after Nostradamus had died.

By 1554, when the plague was thought to be on the retreat, Nostradamus had settled in Marseilles, but that year there were massive floods and the swollen rivers, polluted with infected corpses, carried the disease to every part of the region. Once again Nostradamus found himself working around the clock to ease the suffering of the people. It was remarkable that in his close contact with so many sufferers he never succumbed to the disease himself.

In November 1554 he settled in Salon where he married Anne Ponsart Gemelle, a rich widow. Most of the treasures and rewards which grateful towns had heaped on Nostradamus for his care of plague victims had been given away to the poor, but a comfortable life now seemed a certainty thanks to his wise marriage which provided him with a daughter and three sons, a peaceful home life and no money worries. He converted the top room of his house into a study and began work on his immortal *Prophecies* – the foretelling of the future using all his wisdom, astronomical gifts and occult beliefs. In such an age, when the terror of the (church) Inquisition hung heavily over anyone deemed to be a heretic, Nostradamus was

b xvii Dominica Michadis in mote tula

The sign of Scorpio (**above**) *of the conspicuous southern constellation lying on the ecliptic – the Sun's apparent path through the Heavens – between Sagittarius and Libra.*

certainly taking chances in committing his predictions to paper. He initially composed the prophetic riddles – quatrains – for his own interest; it was only later that he decided to publish them. However, he made sure that they were extremely difficult to interpret, written as they were in a hotchpotch of high French, Provençal French, Italian, Greek and Latin, and riddled with symbolism. Their time sequence was deliberately mixed up so that their meaning and chronology 'would not be immediately discernible to the unwise'. The latter was probably a built-in safeguard in case the guardians of the rack and the branding iron in the Inquisition became displeased with him.

In a section on Nostradamus in his book of seers entitled *They Saw Tomorrow* Charles Neilson Gattey said: 'Even today, when one first reads the original French edition, one's initial reaction is of perplexed disillusion. The language is enigmatic, at times almost unintelligible, as if written in code. The verses are not in chronological order, and jump about in time and subject. Strange soubriquets of Nostradamus' own coining are used for famous personalities. Everywhere we find mystifying puns and anagrams.' But ever since their publication, the *Prophecies* have

withstood the test of time and proved that Nostradamus was an incredible seer.

By 1555 he had completed the first part of his life's work – an almanac of prophecies that were to chronicle world history from his time until the end of the world. The forecasts were called 'The Centuries'; the word 'centuries' had nothing to do with a span of 100 years – it was because there were 100 verses in each book, of which the author intended to write ten. In the preface to the first, Nostradamus wrote that he was afraid that he would be killed by an angry mob if he committed to paper the future which had been revealed to him in prophetic visions. 'That is why I have withheld my tongue from the vulgar and my pen from paper,' he said. 'But later on I thought I would, for the common good describe the most important of the revolutionary changes I foresee, but so as not to upset my present readers I would do this in a cloudy manner with abstruse and twisted sentences rather than plainly prophetical.' Only some of the Centuries are dated – although Nostradamus claimed he could have given a date to all of them had he so wished. Regarding 1792, for instance, when the French Revolution was at its height, he wrote that the year would be 'marked by a far worse persecution of the

Above: *Catherine de Medici, wife of King Henri II of France. She called upon the wisdom of Nostradamus to foresee the future for her sons. He obliged – albeit diplomatically, for fear that too much truth could have cost him his head.*

THE DARK MAGICAL TEXTS HAD SUCH AN INFLUENCE ON HIM THAT HE DECIDED TO BURN THEM IN CASE THEY FELL INTO EVIL HANDS.

Christian Church than ever was in Africa, and which everyone will think an innovation of the age.' That year, Madame Guillotine was at her bloody zenith across France.

At the beginning of his work he also gave the reader an insight into how he divined his prophecies, again in the form of a quatrain: 'Sitting alone at night in secret study; it is placed on the brass tripod. A slight flame comes out of the emptiness and makes successful that which should not be believed in vain.' He went on: 'The wand in the hand is placed in the middle of the tripod's legs. With water he sprinkles both the hem of his garment and his foot. A voice, fear; he trembles in his robes. Divine splendour; the god sits nearby.' According to Nostradamus expert Erika Cheetham in her authoritative work *The Prophecies of Nostradamus*, he touches the middle of the tripod with his wand and then moistens his robe and feet with the water placed on it. 'This is the same method as was used to obtain inspiration by the Apollonian prophetess at the oracles of Branchus in Classical times,' she said. 'Nostradamus is afraid of the power he evokes when it comes to him; he hears it as well as sees it;

it appears to speak to him and he writes down the prophecies. He is unafraid once the gift has possessed him. This dual aspect of his vision is most important when interpreting the centuries.'

Nostradamus also relied heavily on the impressive library he had built up, containing many rare books and manuscripts on the occult. He was influenced by dark, magical texts which he later decided to burn when they came into conflict with his deep religious beliefs. He claimed that when they burned a 'subtle illumination' was cast over his house, acting as a catalyst for further divination and prophecy. He wrote: 'Many occult volumes, which have been hidden for centuries have come into my possession, but after reading them, dreading what might happen if they should fall into the wrong hands, I presented them to Vulcan, and as the fire devoured them, the flames licking the air shot forth an unaccustomed brightness, clearer than natural flame, like the flash from an explosive powder, casting a peculiar illumination all over the house, as if it were wrapped in sudden conflagration. So that you might not in the future be tempted to search for the perfect transmutation, lunar or solar, or for uncorruptible metals hidden under the earth or the sea, I reduced them to ashes.' While using his psychic, meditative and prophetic powers for the Centuries, he was also a firm believer in astrology, using many astrological charts, constellations, planets and signs, to date the quatrains. His implication in the introduction to the Centuries was that, while future events and their dates are determined by planetary movements, their description needed to be modified by the 'spirit of prophecy'.

He ends his introduction to the prophecies by stating that he is not 'vain' enough to call himself a prophet. He says he is a mortal man, 'the greatest sinner in the world, and heir to every human affliction, but, by being surprised sometimes by a prophetical mood, amid prolonged calculation, while engaged in nocturnal studies of sweet odour, I have composed books of prophecies, containing each one a hundred astronomical quatrains which I have joined obscurely and are perpetual vaticinations from now to the year 3797'.

At the end of 1555, the first three Centuries and part of the fourth were published and the fame of Nostradamus spread across Europe with all the speed of the plague that he had devoted his earlier life to conquering. Much of his celebrity spread by word of mouth, from village to village and city to city, as books were expensive and purely a luxury for the rich. But it was at the highest levels of French society where his prophecies aroused most interest, particularly at the court of the royal family. In a superstitious age, someone like Nostradamus was regarded with a mixture of both awe and fear.

Catherine de Medici, wife of Henri II of France, was an avowed occultist, who had entertained many fortune tellers, seers, prophets and charlatans as she tried to plot the course of her beloved husband's reign. She sent for Nostradamus shortly after the publication of the Centuries – both curious and concerned about several passages which, if they were realized, were ominous for the king. It was Quatrain 35 of the first Century which was most worrying, however, as it seemed to predict his death in battle. It read: 'The young lion will overcome the older one, in a field of combat in single fight; He will pierce his eyes in their golden cage; two wounds in one, then he dies a cruel death.' Nostra-

damus arrived in Paris on 15 August 1556 with specific instructions from Catherine de Medici to interpret it.

Catherine was certain of Nostradamus's powers from the first moment she saw him; an aura seemed to emanate from him, particularly from his eyes, and he was adorned with none of the charms and amulets so beloved of the 30,000-odd occultists who made Paris their home. Initially, she hedged around asking him to interpret the quatrains pertaining to the king, instead asking him advice on cosmetics and alternative healing practices. Curiosity, eventually, led her to seek an explanation of the king's death. Nostradamus explained as delicately as he could that he had no power over the visions he had, that he merely recorded events as they came to him. He was aware that a previous seer to the court, a man named Gaurico, had endured horrific torture for prophecies about the king's demise, but he told her anyway – that the king would die in a duel. In 1559 his prediction came true. In celebration of two royal weddings, jousts, tournaments and feasts spanning a three-day period were held in Paris. On the final day the king jousted with Captain Montgomery of the Scottish

Below: *Nostradamus, commanded by Catherine, is depicted here with occult symbols such as the zodiac, a cat and skulls. He is engaged in summoning up pictures of future French kings in a mirror.*

Guard, with both men wearing the emblem of a lion on their chests. When they rode against each other for a third time the splintered end of Montgomery's lance pierced first the king's throat and then knocked up his protective visor, piercing his eye. Mortally injured by the 'two wounds in one', he was carried from the field of combat to die in agony ten days later.

After this, Nostradamus drew up the horoscopes for the royal offspring – children for whom he had already predicted grim fates in the Centuries. Rather than piling on the agony, he diplomatically concentrated on the positive aspects of their lives, predicting that all Catherine's sons would be kings; only François died before he could ascend to the throne.

After his royal audiences he lived in Salon, continuing to work on the Centuries and, upon command, drawing up horoscopes for his many learned and wealthy visitors. In 1564 Catherine, now Queen Regent, went on a royal tour of France with 800 family members, courtiers and attendants. One of her first calls was on Nostradamus, whom she dined with and bestowed upon the privileged title of Physician in Ordinary. It carried with it a small stipend and other benefits; more importantly, it silenced those justices and clergy who mumbled from time

to time about heresy and witchcraft being practised by the old sage.

One interesting incident worth recording occurred during this royal visitation in Salon. Nostradamus, whose visions were the root of his prophecies, also occasionally foretold future events by looking at a person or touching them. He attached great importance to birthmarks upon a person's body, believing them portents of greatness. It was while the royal retinue was at Salon that he made a request to view the naked body of a young boy who was with them – ten-year-old Henri of Navarre – but the boy was shy and feared he would be beaten. The old seer crept into his bedchamber that night and examined the boy as he slept, and found the birthmark he was seeking. Catherine still had two sons in line to the throne but Nostradamus was adamant: the child would be king of France. His prophecy was true – Henri of Navarre became Henri IV of France.

After the royal visitation he worked on completing five more Centuries, bringing the total to eight in all, but the completed works were not off the printing press until 1568, two years after he died. Nostradamus made his will on 17 June 1566 and left a large sum of over 3500 crowns. On 1 July he told his local priest to give him the last

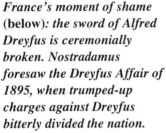

France's moment of shame (below): *the sword of Alfred Dreyfus is ceremonially broken. Nostradamus foresaw the Dreyfus Affair of 1895, when trumped-up charges against Dreyfus bitterly divided the nation.*

rites as he would not be seen alive again. Sure enough, he foretold his own death, with his body being discovered the next morning, a victim of virulent dropsy. He had penned a quatrain for the occasion: 'On returning from an embassy, the King's gift safely stored, No more will I labour, for I will have gone to God, by my close relations, friends and brothers, I shall be found dead, near my bed and the bench.' He lived for 62 years, 6 months and 17 days. His legacy is a work that, through the ages, has been as relevant for people as it was when he was alive. As a prophet, he had the satisfaction of both seeing his predictions come true in his own lifetime as well as having them quoted in the highest circles. Before his death his fame had spread to England where two of his almanacs were printed in London, but it wasn't until 1672 that *The True Prophecies or Prognostications of Michel Nostradamus, Translated and Commentated by Theophilus de Garencieres*, a doctor of the 'College of Physick' in London, were printed, spreading his prophecies to a much wider and altogether more learned audience.

His last request was to be buried upright – he couldn't bear the thought of people walking over him 'during my final sleep'. Placed into the wall of the Church of the Cordeliers in Salon, it was not to be his final grave. In Quatrain 7 of Century IX he had written that evil would come to any man who violated his resting place. It so happened that during the French Revolution the church was pillaged, with one of the looters desecrating his grave, ripping out his skull and using it for a drinking cup. Sure enough, the vagabond was shot dead as soon as he emerged from the crypt. Nostradamus was re-interred in the church of St Laurent in 1813 where he has been allowed to rest in peace ever since. A tablet nearby says: 'Here lie the bones of the illustrious Michel Nostradamus, whose almost divine pen alone, in the judgement of all mortals, was worthy to record, under the influx of the stars, the future events of the whole world. He died at Salon in the year 1566. Posterity, disturb not his sweet rest! Anne Ponce Gemelle hopes for her husband true felicity.' It was written by his second wife.

Although Nostradamus enjoys fame long after his death, he does remain an

enigma to many. In his scholarly work *Oracles of Nostradamus*, author Charles Ward wrote of him: 'It has been well said that the man and his works are an enigma. Everything in our author is ambiguous; the man, the thought, the style. We stumble at every step in the rough paths of his labyrinth. We try to interrogate, but grow silent before a man of emotionless nerve and of impenetrable mask. What are these Centuries? What is Nostradamus? In them and him all may find something; but no man born of woman can find all. The Sphinx of France is here before us; a riddler, riddling of the fate of men; a man at once bold and timid; simple, yet who can plumb his depth? A superficial Christian, a pagan perhaps at heart; a man rewarded of kings; and yet, so far as one can see, furnishing no profitable hint to them that could make their life run smoother or remove a single peril from their path. Behold this Janus of a double face; his very breath is double; the essence of ambiguity lies wrapped incarnate in him and it moulds the man, the thought, the style.'

A villain of the piece in 'L'affaire', as the French termed the Dreyfus scandal, Pierre Waldeck-Rousseau (above) was identified as such in the Centuries.

THE CENTURIES

Only by reading the prophecies – and the violent world events which they seem tailored to – can the enthusiast of Nostradamus really begin to grasp his astonishing powers. There follow some of the most remarkable events that this remarkable individual foresaw, together with interpretations as to their meanings. Some of his more foreboding prophecies, dealing with cataclysmic events yet to come, are left, appropriately, until the end.

CENTURY I, QUATRAIN 7

Arrived too late, the act has been done. The wind was against them, letters intercepted on their way. The conspirators were fourteen of a party. By Rousseau shall these enterprises be undertaken.

TRANSLATION: This is widely regarded as Nostradamus's foretelling of the Dreyfus scandal which rocked France at the turn of this century. Alfred Dreyfus was a Jewish officer of the General Staff falsely accused of passing on vital military intelligence to the arch-enemy, Germany. Nostradamus mentions letters – and indeed, it was later learned, shortly before Dreyfus was pardoned and released from Devil's Island, that faked documents had smeared him in the first place. The term '*vent contraire*' in the language of Nostradamus is interpreted by scholars as meaning political, anti-semitic reasons for his false arrest. But by far the most interesting part of the quatrain is the mention of Rousseau in the last line. Waldeck Rousseau was perhaps the most virulent, violent Dreyfus accuser. And there were, it is believed, no less than 14 generals, staff officers and politicians involved in the conspiracy to brand Dreyfus a traitor.

CENTURY I, QUATRAIN 18

Because of French discord and negligence an opening shall be given to the Mohammedans. The land and sea of Siena will be soaked in blood and the Port of Marseilles covered with ships and sails.

TRANSLATION: In these few words Nostradamus predicted the most cataclysmic event yet to befall mankind – World War 2. The discord is a reference to the chaos which France found herself in during 1940 which allowed the armies of Italy, allied with Hitler, to march into Africa, where their blood was spilled in the desert. The harbour at Marseilles was in German hands and remained a busy port throughout the war.

CENTURY I, QUATRAIN 26

The great man will be struck down in the day by a thunderbolt. An evil deed, foretold by the bearer of a petition. According to the prediction another falls at night time. Conflict at Reims, London and pestilence in Tuscany.

TRANSLATION: This is a prime example of the 'open to interpretation' tag that applies to so many of Nostradamus's predictions, but several historians believe that he is referring to the twin assassinations of the

Kennedy brothers, John and Robert. Gunshots are the 'thunderbolts' with one dying during the day – JFK – and his brother being murdered five years later in June 1968. The petition mentioned could be a reference to the numerous death threats both received while in public life, and the mention of the three places refers to the anguish that swept the world at the news of the deaths.

CENTURY I, QUATRAIN 60

An Emperor will be born near Italy, who will cost the Empire very dearly. They will say, when they see his allies, that he is less a prince than a butcher.

TRANSLATION: Nostradamus predicted the arrival on Earth of Napoleon I, France's greatest warrior son who was indeed born closer to Italy than France upon the island of Corsica. A squanderer of men and resources in his endless campaigns, he cost France dearly in both – hence the additional reference to butchery. Nostradamus had great success in predictions about Napoleon and the Centuries are dotted with references to him.

CENTURY I, QUATRAIN 64

At night they will think they have seen the sun, when they see the half pig man: Noise, screams, battles seen fought in the skies. The brute beasts will be heard to speak.

TRANSLATION: In this remarkable quatrain Nostradamus foresaw a battle in the skies, a totally unique and unknown experience in

NOSTRADAMUS SAW THAT AT FIRST NAPOLEON WOULD BE HAILED AS A GREAT PRINCE, AND THEN AS A BLOODY BUTCHER OF MEN.

How painful it must have been for a true patriot such as Nostradamus to come to terms with his own prophecy foretelling French humiliation at Waterloo (below). Here is Wellington encouraging British troops before the battle.

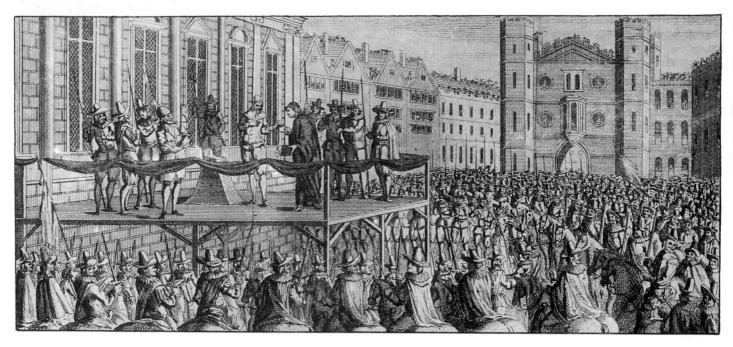

King Charles I (1600–49) on the block (above), *as predicted in Quatrain 49.*

Below: *An engraving of Oliver Cromwell, who was foretold by Nostradamus.*

the times he came from. 'Sun' means searchlight, piercing the sky; pig-like man perfectly sums up the ghoulish appearance of an aviator in goggles and oxygen mask, distending his face like a pig. 'Brute beasts' are the men, speaking to each other over their voice microphones and the

screams may be, according to Cheetham in her work on Nostradamus, the whine of bombs as they fall to Earth.

CENTURY I, QUATRAIN 97

That which neither weapon nor flame could accomplish will be achieved by a sweet speaking tongue in a council. Sleeping, in a dream, the king will see the enemy not in war or of military blood.

TRANSLATION: This relates to the death of Henri III of France in 1589, a monarch who did not die in combat or jousting, but who was assassinated by a monk who pretended he wanted to pass on a message to him. The reference to the dream means the victim will have a premonition of his death – as was the case. Henri III told his royal circle three nights before his murder that he had dreamed of his violent end.

The preceding quatrains give the reader an idea of the style that Nostradamus employed with his predictions. He ranged over the whole gamut of human affairs and emotions: peace and war, love and hate, religion and disbelief.

QUATRAINS ON ENGLAND

In the following sections more of his predictions are grouped according to individual subjects. England was a source of endless intrigue and curiosity for Nostradamus – he believed that the English were to be envied and closely watched at the same time. Perhaps that is why he foresaw so much of how British society would develop.

CENTURY I, QUATRAIN 23
In the third month, at sunrise, the Boar and the Leopard meet on the battlefield. The fatigued Leopard looks up to heaven and sees an eagle playing around the sun.
TRANSLATION: Nostradamus saw the end of Napoleon at Waterloo, the boar signifying the forces of Prussia which teamed up with those of the leopard – England, for Napoleon referred to the British lion on her armed forces' standards as the English Leopard – for the final crushing blow aimed at Boney's ambitions on the Continent. The eagles are those of Napoleon's standards, the Imperial Eagles. The English Leopard is indeed exhausted, but Napoleon knows the end is near.

CENTURY III, QUATRAIN 80
He who had the right to reign in England shall be driven from the throne, his counsellor abandoned to the fury of the populace. His adherents will follow so low a track that the usurper will come to be protector.
TRANSLATION: This prophecy foretold the fall of Charles I. Nothing could be clearer – the king was driven from his throne and his righthand-man Strafford was beheaded. The Scots, his countrymen, sold the king back to Parliament in 1646 for a sum of £400,000 after which Cromwell – referred to in the French version as 'Le bâtard' – became Lord Protector, not the king.

CENTURY IX, QUATRAIN 49
Ghent and Brussels will march past Antwerp, the Senate at London will put their King to death; salt and wine will be applied contrariwise, so that they will set the whole kingdom in disarray.
TRANSLATION: This is the foretelling of the death of Charles I; ironically Quatrain 49, as the king was executed in 1649. Salt and wine was used as a metaphor by Nostradamus for force and wisdom, and is a good example of the vagueness attached to so many of his predictions. The references to the Netherland cities in the first line concerns a war in the Low Countries.

CENTURY VIII, QUATRAIN 76
A butcher more than king rules England. A man of no birth will seize the government by violence. Of loose morals, without faith or law, he will bleed the earth. The hour approaches me so near that I breathe with difficulty.
TRANSLATION: If the preceding quatrain was obscure, then this foretelling of the coming of Oliver Cromwell into English national life could not be clearer. Charles Ward in his work wrote: 'Here we have a most remarkable forecast. It puts into a clear light what view Nostradamus had formed

Queen Victoria (above) *as she appeared in 1876, the empress of a mighty empire upon which the Sun never set. An avowed and ardent royalist, Nostradamus would no doubt have approved of this iron lady of her times.*

Below: *Elizabeth I, England's Virgin Queen, whose 'triumphant' reign was spelled out in Quatrain 74 of Century VI.*

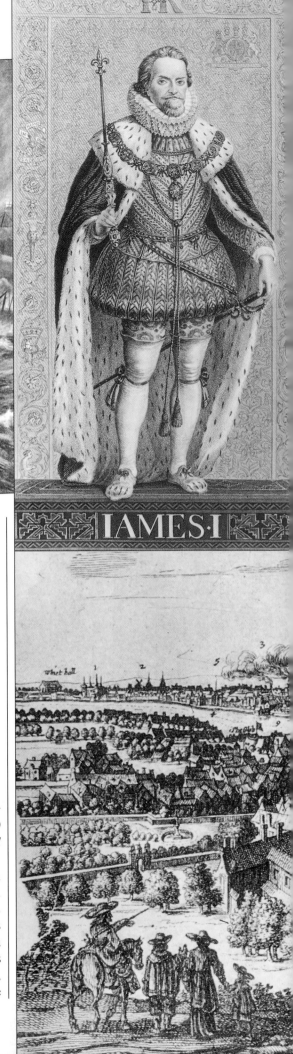

IAMES·I

These floating platforms of Spanish policy and grand design (above) *were broken by the Englishman Francis Drake. But their end had been seen years before by Nostradamus.*

Above right: *James I, whose ascension was foretold in a quatrain which also prophesied massive floods. The master was right on both counts.*

The Great Fire of London as seen from Bankside (right). *Fire consumed the old medieval city for good – and with it much of the splendid architecture of the age.*

of Cromwell. There appears to have been visually present to him the butcher-like face of Cromwell, with its fleshy conch and hideous warts. This seems to have struck him with such a sense of vividness and horror that he is willing to imagine that the time is very near at hand. A full century had, however, to elapse, but he sighs as with a present shudder, and the blood creeps.' It is a departure from the norm in the Centuries in that in it Nostradamus has imparted a sense of the genuine revulsion he felt, giving the reader an idea of how horror-stricken he was when the prophecy came upon him.

CENTURY X, QUATRAIN 100
England the Pempotam will rule the great empire of the waters for more than 300 years. Great armies will pass by sea and land; the Portuguese will not be satisfied.
TRANSLATION: This is the very last quatrain of the last Century but, as stated before, there was no order to the prophecies written down. Most scholars regard this as a statement on the greatness of the British Empire, stretching from Elizabethan times through to the reign of Queen Victoria, when indeed *Pax Britannica* ruled the

waves and the world before modern times sharply reduced her power and influence. Portugal is mentioned because she is Britain's oldest ally in treaties that go back almost 1000 years – although, of course, it was practically half that time ago when Nostradamus penned his prediction. Pempotam is a good illustration of the quasi-classical words that Nostradamus typically peppered his prophecies with – it derives from the Greek *pan*, meaning all, and the Latin *potens*, meaning powerful.

CENTURY IV, QUATRAIN 96

The elder sister of the British Isle shall be born 15 years before her brother; true to her intervening promise, she will succeed to the kingdom of the balance.

TRANSLATION: This means that Mary, elder sister of Edward VI, shall ascend the throne of England. Nostradamus got it slightly wrong here – she was 26, not 15, years older than her brother. She ascended to the throne with the aid of husband William of Orange. The phrase 'kingdom of balance' is one of those pithy comments that often laced the quatrains. In using it, Nostra-

damus draws attention to England's continual quest for a balance of power in Europe and the world, so that no state should outgrow another either militarily or politically and thus threaten stability.

CENTURY VI, QUATRAIN 74

The rejected one shall at last reach the throne, her enemies found to have been traitors. More than ever shall her period be triumphant. At seventy she shall go assuredly to death, in the third year of the century.

TRANSLATION: Elizabeth I was long withheld from the throne – and, of course, when she ascended to it she naturally regarded all those who had kept her from it as enemies and traitors. No reign was ever more triumphant than that of Elizabeth as she defied the might of the Catholic Church in Rome, destroyed the Spanish Armada and seized Spanish lands in the Americas. England flourished as she had never done before with righteous pride in great achievements. And, as Nostradamus predicted, Elizabeth died when she was 70.

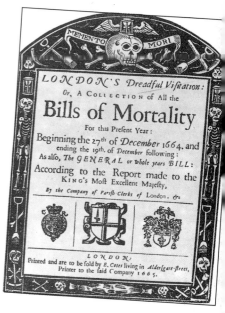

Above: *The Bills of Mortality, a 1665 publication chronicling those who died in an outbreak of plague, one of many that wreaked havoc upon London.*

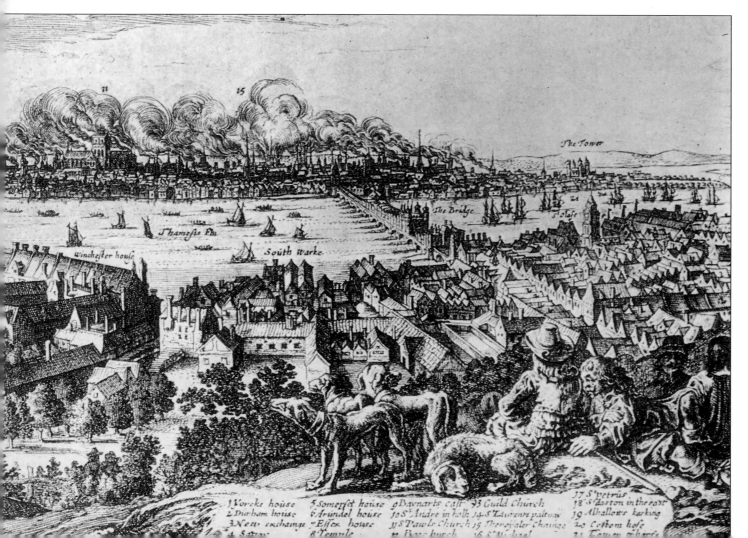

Prince Charles, pictured here in polo outfit (above). *The medieval sage was amazingly accurate when it came to describing the trials and tribulations of the House of Windsor. Only time will tell whether he will be the last British king – if he becomes king at all.*

'THIS MAY MEAN THAT PRINCE CHARLES WILL BE THE LAST KING ON THE BRITISH THRONE.'

CENTURY III, QUATRAIN 70
Great Britain comprising England, will come to be inundated very forcibly by the waters. The new league in Italy will make war such that all band against any one of the cosignatories.
TRANSLATION: England became Great Britain when Scotland was united with her in 1603 at the accession of James I, who assumed the title 'King of Great Britain'. Historians believe the floods Nostradamus speaks of occurred around the end of January 1607, when the sea breached dykes in Somerset and overflowed the countryside. An old Latin book called *Rerum in Gallia, Belgia, Hispania et Anglia* gives details of the disaster, an almost apocalyptic event at the time.

CENTURY II, QUATRAINS 51, 52, 53
The blood of the just shall be required of London, burnt by fireballs in thrice twenty and six; the ancient lady shall fall from its high place and many edifices of the same sort shall be destroyed.
Through many nights the earth shall tremble; in the spring two shocks follow each other: Corinth and Ephesus shall swim in the two seas, war arising between two combatants strong in battle.
The great plague of the maritime city shall not diminish till death is sated for the just blood, basely sold and condemned for no fault. The great Cathedral outraged by feigning saints.
TRANSLATION: Historians by tradition have grouped these three quatrains together when analysing their meaning. The first is an astonishingly accurate description of the Great Fire of London, which happened in 1666, the year Nostradamus predicted. St Paul's is, in the original, taken to be the 'Dame antique' which falls to the flames. The 'just blood' or blood of the just is a reference to the many innocents who died in their wooden homes as the fire, which started in a baker's shop, levelled the medieval city. Nostradamus was no republican; he believed in the divine right of kings and would have seen the fire visited upon London as a fit punishment for the execution of Charles I.

The second quatrain concentrates on the English war with the United Provinces of the Netherlands between 1665 and 1667. 'Cruising' within the narrow channel separating England from Europe, he draws a simile with Aegean waters – Corinth for England, Ephesus for Antwerp.

The third concerns the Black Death, or Great Plague, which devastated London in 1665. 'Maritime city' (due to its dependence on shipping and trade) was a common description of the English capital in use during Nostradamus's day. The outrage he refers to is most probably his own; a confirmed Catholic, he viewed with dismay the protestantism which he foresaw arising in England against the church he loved.

CENTURY IV, QUATRAIN 89
Thirty of London shall conspire secretly against their king; upon the bridge the plot shall be devised. These satellites shall taste of death. A fair-haired king shall be elected, native of Friesland.
TRANSLATION: In 1689 William III – a fair-haired native of Friesland – became king of England after sailing from Holland. It is

interesting to note that when Nostradamus was alive the possibility of a Dutchman taking over the throne of England was as likely as a Soviet politician taking over the White House! Experts estimate that between 30 and 50 opponents of James II conspired to get William on the throne – and that the satellites facing death are his supporters.

CENTURY *III*, QUATRAIN *57*

Seven times you will see the British nation change, dyed in blood for two hundred and ninety years. Not at all free through German support, Aries fears for the protectorate of Poland.

TRANSLATION: The second part is easy enough – Britain going to war for the sake of Poland, as was the case in 1939. It is the first part which vexes historians, wondering when it is that the 290 years starts from. There are some who believe that it is a reference to Prince Charles. Erika Cheetham says: 'This may mean that Prince Charles will be the last King on the British throne.'

CENTURY *VI*, QUATRAIN *41*

The second leader of the kingdom of Annemarc, through those of Frisia and the British Isles, will spend more than one hundred thousand marks, attempting in vain a voyage to Italy.

TRANSLATION: Perhaps rather tenuously, experts believe the reference to Annemarc pertains to Princess Anne and Captain Mark Phillips. At the time of writing England and Frisia had the same ruler – Philip of Spain,

husband to Mary of England and ruler of the Netherlands. In Century IV, Quatrain 27, there is a reference to 'Dannemark' which may be construed as also being about the royal couple – a well-concealed Nostradamus riddle, and one that has yet to be fully understood.

CENTURY *VIII*, QUATRAIN *82*

Thin, tall and dry like reeds, playing the good valet in the end will have nothing but his dismissal, sharp poison and letters in his collar, he will be caught escaping into danger.

TRANSLATION: Her Majesty Queen Elizabeth II was mortified – as was the nation – when the keeper of her royal art collection, Anthony Blunt, was exposed as one of the Oxbridge communist traitor ring which included such notorious agents as Kim Philby and Guy Burgess. He was a trusted official who betrayed his trust at the highest levels.

Above: *The Duke of Windsor and his duchess, formerly Wallis Simpson, the woman for whom he relinquished a crown and an empire.*

Left: *A picture of happiness at the time of their 1973 wedding – Princess Anne and Captain Mark Phillips. The 'Annemarc' quatrain may refer to them but it is still a riddle to experts.*

The great warrior son of France, Napoleon, featured extensively in the predictions. His birthplace is shown (above), together with his retreat from the field at Waterloo (below).

her sister Mary Tudor to the throne. Humble in the days before she became monarch, she nevertheless made up for it with monumental pride during her reign.

CENTURY X, QUATRAIN 22
Not wanting to consent to divorce, afterwards recognized as unworthy, the king of the islands will be forced to flee, and one put in his place who has no sign of kingship.

TRANSLATION: As clear as a bell – the abdication of Edward VIII over his love affair with the divorced American woman, Wallis Simpson. He was forced to leave his homeland because of the establishment's disdainful view of the woman he loved. George VI, who was not in line for the throne, finally became king.

QUATRAINS ON NAPOLEON

Nostradamus gave many predictions for Napoleon, the soldier-statesman who took

CENTURY X, QUATRAIN 19
The day she will be saluted as queen, the prayers coming the day after the blessing. The account is right and valid; once humble, there was never a woman so proud.

TRANSLATION: A reference to Queen Elizabeth I of England, after she succeeded

France to undreamed-of heights in his wars of conquest. An avowed royalist, perhaps the prophet saw in him some of the greatness which he believed France lost after the Revolution of 1789 – something he also foretold. There follows Nostradamus's most amazing predictions on Napoleonic rule – quatrains which, no matter which way they are interpreted, leave no room for misunderstanding about this great warrior-statesman whose arrival he predicted.

CENTURY III, QUATRAIN 35
In the Southern extremity of Western Europe, a child shall be born of poor parents, who by his tongue shall seduce the French army; his reputation shall extend to the Kingdom of the East.
TRANSLATION: Napoleon's birthplace was Corsica, his parents poor and his proclamations of greatness ('*la gloire*') for France and her warriors electrified the troops under his command. The last line may refer to his famous expedition to Egypt or his designs upon the throne of Imperial Russia, which ended in defeat and misery in the winter campaign of 1812.

CENTURY IX, QUATRAIN 33
Hercules, King of Rome and Denmark, surnamed the triple giant of France, shall make Italy tremble and the wave of St Mark, first in renown of all monarchs.
TRANSLATION: In his book, Ward argues that Nostradamus in this quatrain not only predicts the arrival of Napoleon but also the whole Napoleonic dynasty. He says: 'There was a Celtic Hercules fabled to draw men by their ears, but this Hercules means the Napoleonic dynasty. As to King of Rome, Napoleon actually assumed that title, and later on he conferred it upon his son by Marie Louise.'

CENTURY V, QUATRAIN 60
It will have chosen badly in the cropped one, its strength will be sapped badly by him. So great will be the fury and violence that they will say that he is butchering his countrymen with fire and sword.
TRANSLATION: Traces of the bitterness and disenchantment which the French began to feel about Napoleon, after the euphoria of his earlier victories had worn off. Here

there is none of the *élan*, the glory: merely a sense of bitterness and recrimination as Frenchmen die on battlefields all across Europe.

CENTURY X, QUATRAIN 24
The vanquished prince is exiled in Italy, escaped by sea sailing past Genoa and Marseilles. He is then crushed by a massive concentration of foreign armies. Though he escapes the fire the bees will be drained to extinction.
TRANSLATION: Following his flight from Elba, Napoleon landed in the south of France, near Marseilles, where he rallied

At the end it was Napoleon's élite guard (above) *who were all that were left with unflinching loyalty to their emperor. They were truly the last symbols of 'la gloire' that he dreamed of for France.*

Below: *In Notre Dame Cathedral the man whom Nostradamus foresaw as an ominous influence on French affairs takes the step from mortal to demi-god when he proclaims himself emperor.*

troops for the final showdown with foreign armies on French soil. It took place, of course, at Waterloo, where the massed legions of Britain and Prussia decimated him. The bees 'drained to extinction' is a clever touch. The bees being Napoleon's emblem, Nostradamus shows that his ambitions have been thwarted, his power spent, yet he is not dead.

CENTURY VIII, QUATRAIN 61
Never shall he in broad daylight, reach to the symbol of sceptre-bearing rule. Of all his possessions none will be of a settled permanency, conferring of the Gallic cock a gift of the armed legion.

TRANSLATION: This is taken to mean that the Emperor Napoleon will never enjoy a settled seat of firmly established government, but he does bequeath a unique gift to France, one which changed the way nations recruited their forces and the way they fought wars. Until Napoleon's time, armies consisted of professional recruits or mercenaries. Napoleon conscripted huge national armies which effectively made Europe an armed camp – the 'armed legion' of the last line of the quatrain. Some believe there may be a hint in the quatrain in 'settled permanency' to the graveyards of Spain and Portugal where so many of his brave soldiers fell fighting for him.

CENTURY IV, QUATRAIN 26
The great swarm of bees shall rise, that none can tell from whence they came. Night's ambush; the jay beneath the tiles. City betrayed by five tongues not naked.

TRANSLATION: The bees in question stand for the massed ranks of the Napoleonic army, and also his personal emblem which was woven on to embroideries which he carried into battle. Ward believes that the meaning of 'none can tell from whence they came' is a reference to the *bonhomie* and brotherly love engendered by the Revolution – that men are no longer distinct classes, but a single unit united in a common cause. The second part of the quatrain refers to a five-man committee that literally handed Paris over to Napoleon during the coup of 9 November 1797, who were bribed to give way to his consular officers. The coup was planned the night before. In the French, Nostradamus cites the word '*treilhos*' which most interpret as the Tuileries, which became Napoleon's headquarters. Students of Nostradamus are intrigued by this quatrain as it is the only one he wrote in a purely Provençal dialect.

CENTURY VII, QUATRAIN 13
The short-haired man shall assume authority, in maritime Toulon, tributary to the enemy; he will afterwards dismiss as sordid all who oppose him; and for fourteen years direct a tyrant.

TRANSLATION: The English had seized Toulon in the name of Louis XVII and held it for a few months until Napoleon retook

'Not tonight, Josephine', goes the old joke; here (left) the emperor sits with his mistress in an ornate salon as she is attended by a lady-in-waiting.

it. He overturned its government and suppressed free speech in a tyranny which lasted until his overthrow after the battle of Waterloo – a 14-year period. 'Sordid' is generally believed to be a reference to the English, whom Nostradamus believed never had any right to be in France at any time in history.

CENTURY *VIII*, QUATRAIN *57*
From a simple soldier he will rise to the empire, from the short robe he will attain the long. Able in arms, in church government he shows less skill; he raises or depresses the priests as water a sponge.
TRANSLATION: Napoleon was a plain soldier in 1785, consul for life in 1799 and emperor from 1804 until 1814. He changed the formal consular short robe for longer ones. Valiant in battle, he was less skilled in ecclesiastical affairs; nevertheless, he vexed the priests and penetrated into every nook and cranny of their office.

CENTURY *I*, QUATRAIN *88*
He shall have married a woman just before the divine wrath falleth on the great prince; and his support shall dwindle in a sudden atrophy; Counsel shall perish from this shaven head.
TRANSLATION: This is a reference to his infidelity to Marie-Louise of Austria – his wife – with Josephine Beauharnais, his mistress. The shaven head is regarded as an unmistakable reference to Napoleon by Nostradamus experts, relating to the former's close-cropped hair. Counsel perishing from his shaven head alludes to good judgement fleeing Napoleon – perhaps as the result of epilepsy.

Below: *Journey's end for the warrior is Elba – his ultimate exile where spartan living and few home comforts are an unpleasant change from the lifestyle he enjoyed as emperor.*

CENTURY I, QUATRAIN 4
Throughout the universe a monarch shall arise, who will not be long in peace nor life; the bark of St Peter will then lose itself, being directed to its greatest detriment.

TRANSLATION: This is the Emperor Napoleon reviving his pretensions and ambitions to the Holy Roman Empire, but as Nostradamus says, he was doomed to enjoy neither peace, nor life as an emperor, for long. Pope Pius VII first crowned Napoleon as emperor and then became his prisoner when the dictator annexed the Papal States to France in 1809. Religious anarchy existed in France during this time.

Above: *The Russian winter destroyed Napoleon's forces in 1812 as he approached, and then retreated from, Moscow. Nostradamus also successfully predicted the Hitler debacle in Russia a century and a half later.*

Astride Bocephalus, his great white charger (right), Napoleon leads his conquering army to the pyramids, a great wonder of the ancient world.

CENTURY II, QUATRAIN 44

The eagle, drifting in her cloud of flags, by other circling birds is beaten home. Till war's hoarse trumpet and the clarion shrill, recall her senses to the insensate dame.

TRANSLATION: The eagle – the Napoleonic eagle carried by his legions – is in full retreat from the gates of Moscow in the 1812 winter campaign which decimated his legions. The other birds are a reference to the imperial eagles of Russia, Prussia and Austria chasing it all the way back to Paris. The martial music and devastating defeat bring France back to its senses and end in the ultimate defeat of Napoleon.

CENTURY X, QUATRAIN 86

Like a griffon the King of Europe will come, accompanied with those of the north. Of red and white there will be a great number, and they will go against the King of Babylon.

TRANSLATION: The King of Europe is Louis XVII, coming like the mythical griffon, marching with legions dressed in red and white – Austrian and British troops – who will enter Paris, here described as Babylon.

CENTURY VI, QUATRAIN 89

Between two prisons, bound hand and foot, with his face anointed with honey and fed with milk, exposed to wasps and flies, and tormented with the love of his child, his cupbearer will false the cup that aims at suicide.

TRANSLATION: Napoleon, after being consecrated by Pius VII, and anointed with honey and milk, is then imprisoned in Elba and St Helena. The wasps are a reference again to the imperial bees. The two prisons are also taken to mean two wretched states he alternated between after he destroyed his family with his philandering.

CENTURY II, QUATRAIN 99

Roman land as interpreted by the augurs will be greatly molested by the French nation. But the French will come to dread the time of the North wind having driven their fleet too far.

TRANSLATION: In 1812 the ambitions of Napoleon were broken upon the snow-covered steppes of Russia in the campaign that decimated his Imperial Army and his hopes for glory. 'Having driven their fleet

HE DESTROYED HIS FAMILY WITH HIS PHILANDERING.

A cartoon showing the planned Napoleonic onslaught on England (below) – the island of 'shopkeepers' that he was determined to subjugate.

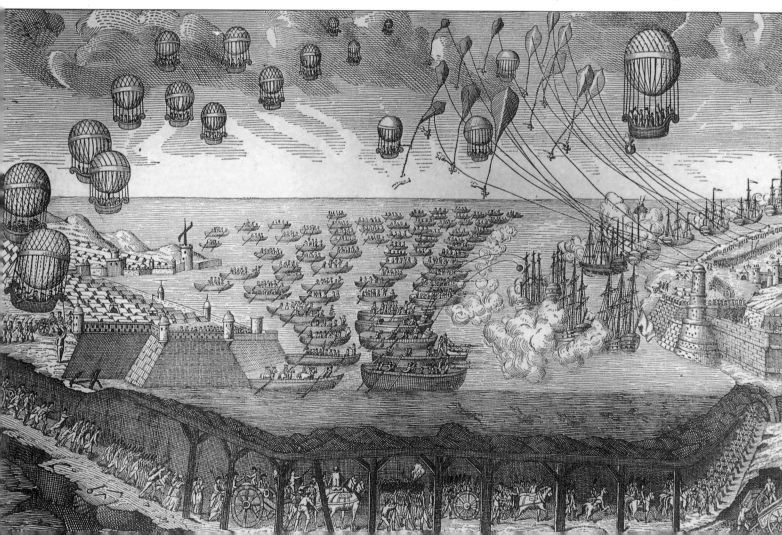

too far' is a clear indication that Napoleon had overextended his forces in his drive on Moscow, the mistake which would be made by that other 'bird of prey', Hitler, nearly a century and a half later. The first part of the quatrain refers to the Vatican States which had been absorbed into the Napoleonic empire in 1810.

CENTURY II, QUATRAIN 29

The oriental will quit his post, to cross the Apennines and see after Gaul. He will transfix the heaven, the mountain ice and snows, striking each of them with his huge magic wand.

TRANSLATION: 'The oriental' is a reference to Napoleon returning to France after his Egyptian expedition, via the Apennines and Alps. Napoleon built marvellous roads through the mountains using his troops, hence the reference to heaven, ice and snows – elements that he kept at bay. His magic wand is nothing more than a huge riding switch that he habitually carried.

CENTURY IV, QUATRAIN 54

Of a name that never belonged to a Gallic king, never was there so terrible a thunderbolt. He made Italy tremble, Spain and the English. He wooed a foreign lady with assiduity.

TRANSLATION: A simple foretelling – one of

Above: *Napoleon at Fontainebleau, from the painting by Paul Delaroche in the Museum of Leipzig. The portrait was painted a year before the emperor's Waterloo defeat.*

A lonely figure, Napoleon strolls in exile upon St Helena (right). *The days of glory are over.*

Left: *The burning ships of Napoleon's Mediterranean fleet at the Battle of Trafalgar. A study of Nostradamus might have dissuaded him from facing the mighty British fleet under Nelson.*

The Iranian royal family **(below).** *The Shah and his queen in the glory days before the Iranian revolution banished the Pahlavi dynasty from the world stage.*

several – of the coming of Napoleon, a man with no name like any other. The foreign lady referred to in the last line is believed to be a reference to Marie-Louise of Austria.

CENTURY VIII, QUATRAIN 53
In Boulogne he would make up for his shortcomings, but cannot penetrate the temple of the Sun. He hastens away to perform the very highest things. In the hierarchy he never had an equal.
TRANSLATION: Over the French seaport of Boulogne towers a column dedicated to Napoleon. From its summit on a clear day visitors can see England – and that is all Boney managed to do, even though he intended to launch his invasion from the shores of Boulogne. Westminster Abbey was built on the site of a pagan Sun temple – the high English church which Napoleon never managed to enter. The 'very highest things' he sought to perform included his vanquishing of the Papal States and his attempted conquest of Russia. And he was without equal in his lifetime.

CENTURY IX, QUATRAIN 86
From Bourg la Reine they shall not come straight to Chartres. They shall camp close to Pont Anthony: seven chiefs for peace, wary as martens, shall enter Paris cut off from its army.

Nostradamus warned of a new force in the Middle East. It came in the shape of the Ayatollah Khomeini (above), whose brand of Islamic fundamentalism swept away the Shah.

IRONICALLY NOSTRADAMUS PREDICTED THE TERRIBLE DANGER THAT THE **CIA** AND THE **KGB** BOTH FAILED TO FORESEE.

Right: *The monster Adolf Hitler – referred to by Nostradamus as 'Hister'. The war he unleashed was chronicled in many of the Centuries.*

TRANSLATION: After the battle of Waterloo and the final defeat of Napoleon, seven nations were drawn to make peace treaties in which it was hoped Europe could live without war and fear. Austria, England, Prussia, Portugal, Sweden, Spain and Russia – the allied nations against Napoleon – entered Paris on 3 July 1815. The city was stripped of its garrison which was sent to Chartres.

CENTURY I, QUATRAIN 98

The general who led infinite hosts, will end his life far from where he was born. Among five thousand people of strange custom upon a chalk island in the sea.

TRANSLATION: Having mapped out his life – his affairs, his battles, his victories and his defeats – Nostradamus successfully foretold the end for France's greatest warrior son. Death came to him far, far from home, upon the island of St Helena, amid people he neither knew nor whose customs he understood.

QUATRAINS ON GREAT WORLD EVENTS

Nostradamus also gave numerous predictions on Napoleonic successors, including Louis XVIII and Louis-Philippe, but it is perhaps his predictions on great world events, events that have shaped the world we inhabit, that arouse the most interest in him. Some are obscure, others could not be plainer. There follows a cross-section of some of his more incredible, perceptive prophecies.

CENTURY I, QUATRAIN 77

A promontory that stands between two seas; a man who will die later by the bit of a horse; Neptune unfurls a black sail for his man; the fleet near Gibraltar and the Rocheval.

TRANSLATION: Standing between the Mediterranean and the Atlantic is the promontory of rock called Gibraltar. Rocheval is an old French word for Cape Roche. It was between Cape Roche and Gibraltar that the greatest British victory at sea, which determined British policy for a number of years to come, occurred in 1805. In that engagement Lord Nelson, deploying superior skills, destroyed the French fleet. A year later Admiral Villeneuve, one of the French commanders on the day, was strangled at a remote French country inn by someone using the bridle of a horse as a weapon. The black sail

Left: *Geneva, 1926: the League of Nations tries to bring together nations with differing opinions so that war may become a thing of the past.*

The bomb-ravaged streets surrounding St Paul's in London (below). Nostradamus was tragically correct in his prophecy of a new kind of war from the air.

General Winter, the most fearsome opponent of them all, halts and destroys German troops in the advance on the Soviet Union (above).

Opposite: The bright, shining hope of the Western world on his inauguration day in 1961. Nostradamus saw his coming – and his tragic departure.

unfurled on the day of the battle was aboard HMS *Victory*, Nelson's flagship, to commemorate the loss of the commander-in-chief.

CENTURY I, QUATRAIN 70
Rain, famine and war will not cease in Persia; too great a trust will betray the monarch. The actions started in France will end there, a secret sign for one to be sparing.

TRANSLATION: It is bitterly ironic to think that the intelligence agencies of the Western world, including the mighty CIA and KGB, could not predict the end of the Peacock Throne in Iran whereas a man who died half a millennium ago could. In this remarkable vision, Nostradamus saw events unfolding centuries beyond his own time that seemed impossible right up to the time they happened. It was a disbelieving world which watched the Shah of Iran being toppled by the religious leader, the Ayatollah Khomeini, in 1979. Rain, famine and war – and all their ensuing misery – partly caused the Shah to be overthrown, but it was in France that the exiled Ayatollah plotted for years for the religious fundamentalist state to take over from the Pahlavi dynasty. The 'sparing' referred to at the end is interpreted as 'spartan' – certainly a fitting description for the new order which currently reigns in Iran.

CENTURY I, QUATRAIN 34
The bird of prey, flying to the left, before battle is joined with the French, he makes preparations. Some will regard him as good, others bad or uncertain. The weaker party will regard him as a good omen.

TRANSLATION: Throughout the Centuries there are several references to World War 2 and to Adolf Hitler, but this is the first clear portent of the fate to come for mankind. The bird of prey is used by Nostradamus to describe both Napoleon and Hitler – both conquerors of different ages. His reference to the bird flying to the left is a clever one; to the left of France are the Low Countries, through which Hitler launched his mechanized armies in an entirely new form of warfare, the Blitzkrieg, in 1940. The references to the good, bad and uncertain are interpreted as descriptions of the weak and divided French governments in the final days of the Third Republic.

CENTURY II, QUATRAIN 100
In the islands shall be such horrible tumult, that nothing shall be heard except a warlike surprise. So great shall be the attack of the raiders, that everyone shall shelter himself under the great line.

TRANSLATION: This suggests the use of incendiaries and other air-dropped bombs being used on great cities, particularly London, in World War 2, where the inhabitants sheltered from the nightly firestorms in the underground rail system.

CENTURY I, QUATRAIN 47
The speeches of Lake Leman will become angered, the days will drag out into weeks, then months, then years, then all will fail. The authorities will condemn their useless powers.

TRANSLATION: At the end of World War 1 – which, incidentally, Nostradamus also correctly predicted – the combatant nations came together in the belief that a new family of countries was necessary, to bind itself to the aims of perpetual peace instead of future possible wars. The League of Nations first met in Geneva in 1920 – the city which sits on the shores of Lake Leman. With penetrating insight in a few short lines, Nostradamus seems to sum up the futility, the bickering and squabbling which defined the League in its few short years of operation before it dissolved in

The Cuban missile crisis in 1962 brought the world to the brink of nuclear annihilation. And yet it had all been witnessed by Nostradamus five centuries before! Shown here (right) is an intermediate-range ballistic missile base in Cuba.

acrimony before the onset of World War 2. In Quatrain 85 of Century V, Nostradamus further cements his vision of a failed league when he writes: 'Through the Swiss and surrounding areas they will war because of the clouds. A swarm of marine locusts and gnats, the faults of Geneva laid quite bare.'

CENTURY II, QUATRAIN 38
There will be a great number of condemned people when the monarchs are reconciled. But one of them will be so unfortunate that they will hardly be able to remain allied.
TRANSLATION: Shortly before the outbreak of World War 2, a pact was struck between Hitler and Stalin which pledged that each would not attack the other. It was a devastating pact with enormous implications for world peace. No one believed that the architects of the two great totalitarian states, one fascist, one communist, could work together. However, Nostradamus clearly saw this reconciliation of modern-day monarchs – and the great number of innocents who were murdered on both sides. Finally, the partners in crime fell out in 1942 with Hitler's massive attack on the USSR – his avowed quest since the earliest days of the Nazi party.

CENTURY II, QUATRAIN 24
Beasts wild with hunger will cross the rivers, the greater part of the battlefield will be against Hister. He will drag the leader in a cage of iron, when the child of Germany observes no law.
TRANSLATION: This is the German who observed no law – Adolf Hitler. It was he who loosed his beasts 'wild with hunger' across the river boundaries of Europe and

the USSR, pillaging, murdering and destroying everything in his path. Dragging leaders in a cage of iron is a reference to old medieval practices of humiliating defeated rulers. Hitler humiliated the conquered lands under his swastika in a more sophisticated manner. Critics have argued among themselves over the years whether Nostradamus actually meant a man called Hister or whether he knew he was called Hitler and disguised his true identity, as he was wont to do in so many of his predictions. One thing is certain: the Führer himself was convinced that Nostradamus meant him and great propaganda was made from this quatrain in the years before he embarked on his crusade which would end in millions of deaths.

CENTURY II, QUATRAIN 1
Towards Aquitaine, by British assaults, and by them also great incursions. Rains and frost make the terrain unsafe, against Port Selin they will make mighty invasions.
TRANSLATION: In 1915, utilizing a plan

drawn up by Winston Churchill, the allies embarked on a perilous expedition which, had it succeeded, could well have shortened World War 1, with all its misery and death, by several years. The allies launched an assault on Turkey – the port of Constantinople was known as Selin in the time of Nostradamus – hoping to bypass the Western Front, with all its misery of frost, rain and snow. Again, this is a remarkable example of the powers of Nostradamus. The plan was scoffed at by the high command – even more so in hindsight when the bloodied remnants of the British and empire forces retreated after being held at bay by the Turks at the Dardanelles straits.

CENTURY II, QUATRAINS 56, 57
One whom neither plague nor sword could kill will die on the top of a hill, struck from the sky. The abbot will die when he sees the ruin of the people in the shipwreck trying to hold on to the reef.
Before the battle the great man will fall,

Above: *A Russian soldier sits in the fetid, waterlogged bunker that was the last headquarters – and the suicide location – of Adolf Hitler in May 1945. But Nostradamus suggests that Der Führer may have lived after the collapse of his Third Reich.*

the great one to death, death too sudden and lamented. Born imperfect, it will go the greater part of the way; near the river of blood, the ground is stained.

TRANSLATION: Historians and enthusiasts of the occult have pored over these two quatrains for many years. Most concur that they refer to the killing of John F. Kennedy, although opinion is divided. Nostradamus chronicler Erika Cheetham says: '*Mort trop subite* in the original probably implies an assassination and *nay imparfaict* a person born with a physical deformity. Senator Kennedy was born with a congenital illness. Many of John F. Kennedy's critics agree that he had a great deal of charisma but wonder whether his political judgement would have been sound had he lived to serve another term of office. "It will go the greater part of the way" may well refer to Kennedy's stand against Khrushchev's attempt to set up missile bases in Cuba. The Russian fleet did, after all, get the greater part of the way from Russia. It was after this confrontation that Kennedy was killed at Dallas.'

CENTURY *III*, QUATRAIN *58*
and CENTURY *IX*, QUATRAIN *90*
Near the Rhine from the Noricum Mountains will be born a great man of the people, born too late. He will defend Poland and Hungary and they will never know what became of him.

The Vichy traitors (above). **As well as seeing the rise of Hitler, Nostradamus chronicled the treachery of Pétain and Admiral Darlan.**

Right: *Israel's prime minister David Ben Gurion, (centre left, wearing jacket), is at the dockside in Haifa in 1948 to see the last British soldier leave the Holy Land's soil.*

A leader of Great Germanies who will come to give help which is only counterfeit. He will stretch the borders of Germany and will cause France to be divided into two parts. Living fire and death hidden in globes will be loosed, horrible and terrible, by night the enemy will reduce cities to dust.

TRANSLATION: In these two quatrains Nostradamus again gives clear, undisguised warnings of the advent of Adolf Hitler and the terrible revenge he will exact on mankind. The globes he refers to are obviously a reference to bombs falling on cities like London and Berlin, the product of his vicious war. Defending Poland and Hungary – he actually attacked them – could be part of Nostradamus's usual trick of trying to be cryptic about actual events. The final line is interesting in the first quatrain; it could imply that Hitler LIVED after the fall of Berlin. Certainly there has been much dispute about whether or not he and mistress Eva Braun died in the ruins of the bunker as the Russians closed in.

CENTURY III, QUATRAIN 71
Those besieged in the islands for a long time will take strong measures against their enemies. Those outside, overcome, will die of hunger, by such starvation as has never occurred before.

TRANSLATION: This is Nostradamus's way of painting a portrait of embattled Britain at war, blockaded by the U-boats as she builds up her war machine and the resolve of the leaders and the people for total victory over the axis powers grows stronger. The references to those outside and the starvation they suffer is seen as a twofold thing: the starvation and deprivation in conquered Europe and in the concentration camps, and also the starvation of the soul, deprived as it was of love, compassion and religious beliefs under the edicts of the Third Reich.

CENTURY III, QUATRAIN 75
Pau, Verona, Vicenza, Saragossa, swords dripping with blood from distant lands. A very great plague will come with the great shell, relief near but the remedies far away.

TRANSLATION: In 1976 in Seveso, Italy, occurred one of the worst man-made disasters in history. A massive chemical plant explosion destroyed wildlife, contaminated drinking water and agricultural land and caused women to give birth to deformed babies. The cloud of gas drifted across a large section of Italy – but, interestingly enough, the towns that Nostradamus wrote about were not affected, nor was the plan to combat the disaster formulated in them. Much of the land is still unusable, proving that the remedies are indeed still far away.

CENTURY III, QUATRAIN 100
The man least honoured among the French will be victorious over his enemy. Strength and lands he explored in action, when suddenly the jealous party dies from a shot.

TRANSLATION: Recognizing the coming of Charles de Gaulle, a man virtually unknown in France before the collapse of the Third Republic, was a remarkable feat. Strength, in terms of political power and prestige, was gathered during his years in exile as the war raged in various countries, and the envious one dying from a shot is thought to be the traitorous appeaser of the Germans, Admiral Darlan, killed on 24 December 1942. Like Hitler and Napoleon, the quatrains are peppered with references to De Gaulle, supporting many believers' contentions that Nostradamus excelled in prophesying the coming of great men upon the world stage.

A peek at freedom. Through a crack in the Berlin Wall (above) an eastsider gazes through to the West in the days before it was torn down for good.

THE PROPHECY IMPLIES THAT HITLER LIVED AFTER THE FALL OF BERLIN.

Right: *The hero of Verdun, Marshal Philip Pétain, was the traitor of Vichy in World War 2. He agreed to co-operate with the Nazis.*

The mighty Rhine (below), *the 'Great River' which Nostradamus referred to in his prophecy about the French Maginot Line.*

CENTURY *III, QUATRAIN 97*
A new law will occupy a new land around Syria, Judaea and Palestine. The great barbarian empire will crumble before the century of the Sun is finished.
TRANSLATION: No one could have foretold in this century, let alone in his day, the creation of the state of Israel in exactly the spot where it would eventually be born in the wake of World War 2, but that is precisely what Nostradamus accomplished. However, part of the prophecy remains unfinished. Nostradamus tags the Arab countries around Israel as 'barbarian' and warns that they will be finished by the end of the 20th century – the century of the Sun.

CENTURY *IV, QUATRAIN 32*
In those times and areas where the flesh gives way to fish, the common law will be

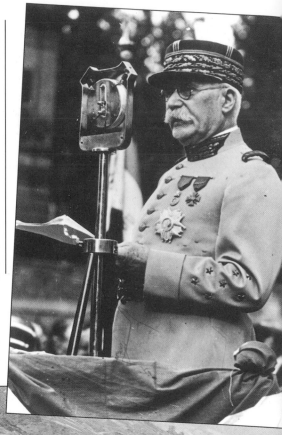

made in opposition. The old order will hold strong then be removed from the scene entirely, all things common among friends put far behind.

TRANSLATION: Communism falls. Nostradamus did not specify in which country, but it is interesting that the system has effectively collapsed in the USSR. Dried fish, as opposed to fresh meat, was a staple of the grumbling peasants under the communist regime. 'All things common among friends' – i.e., communism and the community spirit it was intended to engender among the proletariat – are broken. In other quatrains Nostradamus foretells an alliance that Russia will make, possibly with the USA. Some already believe that this has happened, interpreting 'alliance' as the business deals that are now taking place due to the fall of the old order.

CENTURY IV, QUATRAIN 61
The old man, mocked and deprived of his position by the foreigner who will suborn him. The hands of his sons are devoured before his face, he will betray his brother at Chartres, Orléans and Rouen.

TRANSLATION: With this quatrain Nostradamus paints one of his clear pictures – about Marshal Pétain, the former hero of Verdun who disgraced his nation in World War 2 by becoming the puppet head of Vichy France, the vassal state of Nazi Germany. During his time as premier he was referred to contemptuously by his subjects as 'The Old Man'. The three French cities mentioned were all liberated by the Allies on the same day, and held strong connections with the old France of Nostradamus's times. Interestingly, each one is the site of some of France's most celebrated and mystical cathedrals, all of which were visited by Nostradamus during his travels and from where he drew divine inspiration for the prophecies.

CENTURY IV, QUATRAIN 80
Near the great river, a great trench, earth excavated, the water will be divided into fifteen parts. The city taken, fire, blood, cries and battle given, the greater part concerned with the collision.

TRANSLATION: Before World War 2 France poured the greatest part of her military

The Maginot Line (above). Upon this line of pillboxes and forts France gambled her national security – and lost in 1940 when Hitler's panzers merely went around the side of it.

Right: *The ruins of Paris after the Commune uprising of 1871. The city Nostradamus loved was virtually destroyed.*

Charles de Gaulle, saviour of France (below), in London in 1940 following the shattering news that France and Germany had signed an armistice.

resources, and her national faith, into a static defence line named after a World War 1 engineer called André Maginot. The line stretched from near the Rhine – 'the great river' – across her north-eastern borders, petering out at the start of the Ardennes forest, which the French high command deemed too thick for armour or artillery to operate in. Ironically, in an earlier quatrain, Nostradamus had already predicted this by pointing out that France's enemies would advance through countries to her left – i.e., the low countries of the Netherlands and Belgium. The collision he refers to is the clash of armies throughout the war.

CENTURY IV, QUATRAIN 100

Fire will fall from the sky on to the royal building when the light of war is weakened. For seven months a great war, people dead through evil, Rouen and Evreux will not fail the king.

TRANSLATION: Nostradamus here predicted the Franco-Prussian War of 1870–71 which sowed the seeds of permanent bitterness between the peoples of France and Germany. The war lasted PRECISELY seven months, during which time a fierce siege of Paris laid waste to many royal buildings. The reference to the Normandy towns of Rouen and Evreux is because they did not become republican along with the rest of France after the war, preferring instead to support a restored monarchy.

CENTURY V, QUATRAIN 45

The great empire will soon be desolate, transformed near the forest of the Ardennes. The bastards will be beheaded by the oldest, Aenodarb will rule, the hawknosed one.

TRANSLATION: This foretells the fall of France in 1940, coming as it did via the German advance through the Ardennes forest which the French generals perceived as impenetrable. The bastards are believed to be the two senior French commanders who thoroughly botched battlefield attempts to stem the onrushing tide of German armour, although they were not beheaded, merely captured. The hawknosed one is a reference to General de Gaulle, although no one has found a satisfactory explanation for the classical name Aenodarb.

CENTURY V, QUATRAIN 94

He will change into the Greater Germany, Brabant and Flanders, Ghent, Bruges and Boulogne. The truce feigned, the great Duke of Armenia will assault Vienna and Cologne.

TRANSLATION: Again, this is a quatrain concerning Hitler and, more specifically, his designs of conquest upon the world. The 'feigned truce' is seen as the lame excuse he gave to the world upon his invasion of Poland – that he was merely aiding 'ethnic Germans' persecuted by the Poles. The Duke of Armenia is seen as the Russians who, towards the end of the war, invaded Germany from the south and east.

CENTURY VI, QUATRAIN 72

Through feigned fury of a divine emotion the wife of the great one will be badly violated. The judges wishing to condemn such a doctrine, the victim is sacrificed to the ignorant people.

Above: *Gregori Rasputin, the 'Mad Monk' of the Russian imperial court, whose dominance of the Czarina Alexandra led ultimately to the demise of the Romanov family.*

The Great Dictator, Benito Mussolini (above). His brand of Fascism would lead Italy into ruinous, bloody war.

TRANSLATION: In this Nostradamus has summed up the plight of the Czarina Alexandra, wife of Czar Nicholas, who became spellbound by the evil monk Rasputin. Rasputin exerted a terrible grip on the Russian court, and thereby Russian life, due to his hocus-pocus about her son's haemophilia which she believed. The 'ignorant people' are the masses with whom the Romanov family were so utterly and so completely out of touch, which led to the Russian Revolution, their downfall and murder.

CENTURY VI, QUATRAIN 31
The king will find that which he desires so greatly; when the Prelate will be wrongfully taken. The reply to the Duce will make him angry; in Milan he will put several to death.
TRANSLATION: The foretelling of the rise to power of Mussolini – together with the title of Duce which he conferred upon himself. In Milan several of Mussolini's opponents were exiled while the Prelate, taken to be the Pope, finds himself in a Catholic country surrounded by the forces of the anti-Christ.

CENTURY VIII, QUATRAIN 80
The blood of innocents, widow and virgin, with many evils committed by the Great Red One, holy images placed over burning candles, terrified by fear, none will be seen to move.
TRANSLATION: In 1917 the Romanov dynasty, which had ruled Holy Russia, was swept away in a great revolution that used the colour red for its flag. The blood of innocents could pertain to the children of the royal household, who were massacred along with czar and czarina, or the many millions that died in the ensuing terror after the Bolsheviks took power. Organized religion, bedrock of the czarist regime, was also outlawed in the new order as prescribed by the followers of Lenin. Some interpret the last line as being about the massacre of the royal family at Ekaterineburg in 1917. 'None will be seen to move' may mean that Nostradamus saw that all were murdered, giving the lie to a woman who, for years afterwards until her death in the late 1980s, claimed she was the Princess Anastasia who escaped from the execution site.

CENTURY IX, QUATRAIN 16
From Castel Franco will bring out the assembly, the ambassadors will not agree and cause a schism. The people of Riviera will be in the crowd, and the great man will be denied entry to the great Gulf.

The last czar, Nicholas II, with his son Alexis, the Czarina Alexandra and his nephew Nikita Alexandrovitch (left). Soon they would all be consumed by the great Red Revolution.

Below left: *Is this the Grand Duchess Anastasia, who somehow escaped the massacre that befell her parents and siblings? Or is she in fact an impostor who lived a lie all her life?*

TRANSLATION: This is another of those extraordinarily perceptive prophecies in which the master makes no attempt at disguising his portent for the future. In this he warns of the coming of Franco and the Spanish Civil War. The reference to 'the great man being denied entry' refers to Franco's inability to cross the Mediterranean when he was exiled to Morocco. Gattey writes: 'Ingenious commentators have surmised that the personages named are the late General Franco and his predecessor, the dictator Primo de Rivera, and that the verse also refers to the struggle for power between the two men. The last line alludes to Franco's exile in Morocco, or to his meeting on 12th February 1941 with Mussolini on the Riviera, when he refused to permit the troops of the Axis to pass through Spain and attack Gibraltar. The "great Gulf" is the Mediterranean.'

Nostradamus foresaw the Spanish Civil War and Franco's dictatorship in the earlier Quatrain 54 of Century III. He wrote:

One of the great ones shall fly into Spain which will then bleed with a long

Right: *Another of the great European dictators so successfully foreseen by Nostradamus. Here General Franco makes a tour of the party faithful.*

Divining new methods of war in all their grotesque horror seemed to be a special gift belonging to Nostradamus. Here (below) *are men of the East Lancashire Regiment in a trench at Givenchy in World War 1.*

wound. Armies will pass by the high mountains, destroying all, after which he will reign in peace.

CENTURY IX, QUATRAIN 11
They will come to put the just man wrongfully to death, publicly in the midst he is extinguished. So great a plague will be born in this place that the judges will be forced to flee.

TRANSLATION: This tells of the execution of Charles I of England – while giving an insight again into Nostradamus's belief in the divine right of kings. Charles was beheaded in 1649. The second part of the quatrain is the Great Plague of London which came in 1665. Nostradamus believed that the plague was God's retribution against the men who had overthrown the king.

CENTURY IX, QUATRAIN 55

The dreadful war which is prepared in the west, the following year pestilence will come, so horrible that neither young, nor old, nor animal will survive. Blood, fire, Mercury, Mars, Jupiter in France.

TRANSLATION: Another two-in-one quatrain in which he successfully foretells World War 1 – the war in the west, or Western Front – and the massive influenza outbreak across Europe which followed it, which claimed more lives than the fighting. The planetary references refer to their position at the time the prediction would come true – again, correctly.

CENTURY IX, QUATRAIN 77

The kingdom is taken, the king will plot while the lady is taken to death by these sworn by lot. They will refuse life to the queen's son and the mistress suffers the same fate as the wife.

TRANSLATION: Erika Cheetham believes this to be one of his more 'impressive' quatrains. She writes: 'After the [French] royal family's imprisonment, Louis XVI was executed in January 1793. He was condemned by the convention who elected these powers to itself. However, the queen, who was not executed until the following October, had a newly created Revolutionary tribunal elected to judge her, which was selected by lot. This was an institution unknown to France in Nostradamus' day. The third line tells the fate of Louis XVII. Whether he died or lived abroad is irrelevant; his kingdom was denied to him. Finally, the most interesting line of all. While the queen was imprisoned in the Conciergerie, the old mistress of Louis XV, Mademoiselle du Barry, was taken for a while to the prison of Sainte Pelagie.'

Above: *The end for Marie Antoinette, extravagant bride of the king of France. Here the Dauphin is torn from her before she is led away to her own execution.*

'**PESTILENCE WILL COME, SO HORRIBLE THAT NEITHER YOUNG, NOR OLD, NOR ANIMAL WILL SURVIVE.**'

New warfare; the Japanese attack at Pearl Harbor (above). It crippled America's Pacific fleet in 1941, but ultimately led to Japan's unconditional surrender in 1945.

Opposite: *Halley's Comet, the extra-terrestrial orb which Nostradamus refers to in several quatrains through the Centuries.*

CENTURY IX, QUATRAIN 100
A naval engagement will be overcome by night; fire in the ruined ships of the west. A new code, the great coloured ship, anger to the vanquished and victory in a mist.
TRANSLATION: This describes the attack on Pearl Harbor, 7 December 1941, in which the greater portion of the American Pacific Fleet was destroyed in a surprise attack launched before dawn by a Japanese carrier-borne force. The new coding is believed to refer to aircraft launched from ships, a new kind of war which eventually led to the Allies' victory over Japan.

THE SHAPE OF THINGS TO COME

What does the future hold for us, as defined in the writings of Nostradamus? Even the

most hardened sceptic must concede that the old sage has had some remarkable successes in interpreting the ages. There follows a selection of some prophecies yet to be realized – culminating in those which could spell doom for mankind if the sleeping seer of Salon got them right.

CENTURY II, QUATRAIN 91
At sunrise a great fire will be seen, noise and light extending to the north. Within the globe death and cries are heard, death awaiting them through weapons, fire and famine.
TRANSLATION: Erika Cheetham believes this to be the portent of a great war between Russia and the USA. Although the threat of nuclear confrontation has abated since the fall of the Berlin Wall and the collapse of communism, many observers think that the

situation is still too volatile to predict lasting peace. If this can be linked with Century II, Quatrain 46, it is ominous indeed. That one states:

After great misery for mankind an even greater approaches when the great cycle of the centuries is renewed. It will rain blood, milk, famine, war and disease. In the sky will be seen a fire, dragging a great trail of sparks.

TRANSLATION: Halley's Comet is obviously the fire in the sky with the sparks trailing behind. It is due to appear again at the end of the century – hopefully without the rain of 'blood, milk, famine, war and disease', which some think could be a third world war.

CENTURY IV, QUATRAIN 99

The brave, elder son of a king's daughter will drive the Celts back far. He will use thunderbolts, so many and in such an array, few and distant, then deep into the west.

TRANSLATION: Celts are taken to mean the French. Not being part of NATO, does Nostradamus predict a new tyrant within Europe ready to use thunderbolts – possibly nuclear or chemical missiles – to seize the unprepared French?

CENTURY V, QUATRAIN 90

In the Cyclades, in Perinthus and Larissa, in Sparta and all of the Peloponnesus, a very great famine, plague through false dust. It will last nine months throughout the whole peninsula.

TRANSLATION: Nostradamus is usually very specific about plagues or famines. Here he talks of 'false dust', i.e., possibly man-made, which has led many to believe that this could be a reference to chemical or biological warfare. The Balkans have long been a troublespot in the world – World War 1 was sparked off over them and, more recently, the bloody civil war between Bosnia and Serbia has been fought over parts of the area.

CENTURY VI, QUATRAIN 5

A great famine, the result of a pestilence that will extend its long rain the length of

Endless suffering – Canadian engineers, part of a UN peacekeeping contingent (below), in the killing fields of Bosnia.

the Arctic pole. Samarobrin one hundred leagues from the hemisphere; they will live without law, exempt from politics.

TRANSLATION: Samarobrin has yet to be defined, but most analysts concur that Nostradamus is back to his theme of a chemical fallout on the Earth, possibly emanating from far out in space. Some argue that he foresees a manned space station, where people will indeed live without politics and normal laws, and whose use is corrupted to rain down death on the people below.

CENTURY VI, QUATRAIN 97

The sky will burn at forty-five degrees, fire approaches the great New City. Immediately a huge, scattered flame leaps up when they want to have proof of the Normans.

TRANSLATION: If this one is true then New Yorkers must fear a massive aerial bombing at some point which will destroy most of the metropolis. New York County actually lies between the 40° and 45° parallel in the USA. The last line is typically muddled and no one seems to have come up with a satisfactory explanation of his reference to 'the Normans'.

CENTURY VI, QUATRAIN 24

Mars and the Sceptre will be in conjunction, a calamitous war under Cancer. A short time afterwards a new king will be anointed who will bring peace to the earth for a long time.

TRANSLATION: Seen by most as another reference to war towards the end of this century – but this one more hopeful, with the promise of a new peacemaker to give Earth some respite.

CENTURY VIII, QUATRAIN 9

While the eagle is in unison with the cockerel at Savona, the eastern sea and Hungary. The army at Naples, Palermo, the marches of Ancona, Rome and Venice a great outcry by the Barbarian.

TRANSLATION: Here Nostradamus warns of a Moslem invasion of Italy, naming key Italian cities as targets for the hordes. Italy, home to the Church of Rome, would make a key target for religious fundamentalists seeking to exert domination over the Christian church. And with the rise of

Islamic fundamentalism around the world it is not too far-fetched a prophecy.

CENTURY VIII, QUATRAIN 81

The new empire in desolation will be changed from the Northern pole. From Sicily will come such trouble that it will bother the enterprise tributary to Philip.

TRANSLATION: This tells of a civilization moving southwards, shifting the centre of power in a world region – possibly North America – leading some to believe it will occur after a nuclear holocaust as people look for new life and sustenance in

Above: *The Statue of Liberty at the entrance to the New York harbour. If Nostradamus has got it right the Big Apple will one day burn under a massive aerial bombardment.*

unaffected zones. The references to Sicily and Philip imply that the war might emanate from there or Spain – once ruled by King Philip. This might link up with Century VIII, Quatrain 9, concerning the Moslem invasion of Italy. If Moslem fundamentalists rule this part of Europe perhaps Nostradamus is implying that nuclear war may be triggered in the future.

CENTURY IX, QUATRAIN 83

The Sun in twenty degrees of Taurus, there will be a great earthquake; the great theatre full up will be ruined. Darkness and trouble in the air, on sky and land, when the infidel calls upon God and the saints.

TRANSLATION: Twenty days after the Sun moves into Taurus is 10 April, so Nostradamus gives us the date of a catastrophic earthquake – one which modern-day scientists believe must apply to the San Andreas fault, and more specifically to the destruction of San Francisco, which all experts say MUST happen – it is merely a question of when.

CENTURY X, QUATRAIN 67

A very great trembling in the month of May, Saturn in Capricorn, Jupiter and Mercury in Taurus. Venus also in Cancer, Mars and Virgo, then hail will fall greater than an egg.

TRANSLATION: Nostradamus displays his extensive knowledge of the planets in this quatrain, describing a rare event in the heavenly bodies when all fall into place in a set pattern. Astrologers say the planets will not be in conjunction in this manner until May 3755. Then the world can expect massive earthquakes, followed by enormous hailstones.

CENTURY X, QUATRAIN 72
In the year 1999 and seven months there will come from the skies the Great King of Terror. He will bring back to life the great King of the Mongols. Before and after war reigns happily.

TRANSLATION: It is perhaps fitting – if not sombre – to end a study of Nostradamus upon his most melancholy, unfulfilled prophecy. He tells of an Asian anti-Christ, steeped in the traditions of the warrior hordes of the Mongols, visiting death and destruction upon the face of the globe. Most experts believe that this new demon will be an anti-Christ, committed to tearing down the values of Judaeo-Christian society as we know them. If Napoleon and Hitler were the two other anti-Christ figures that Nostradamus draws in some of his prophecies, then this will be the third and final one.

He makes a further reference to this in Century VIII, Quatrain 77. In that he writes:
The anti-Christ very soon annihilates the three, seven and twenty years his war will last. The unbelievers are dead, captive, exiled: with blood, human bodies, water and red hail covering the earth.

This implies that the third anti-Christ, after Napoleon and Hitler – the one yet to come – will be annihilated, but that it will take 27 years of fearsome war to do so. The reference to red hail could mean atomic fallout, such as that which blanketed the Japanese cities of Hiroshima and Nagasaki after the dropping of the atom bombs towards the close of World War 2.

Although Nostradamus signals the end of civilization as we know it, there could be hope still. In Century I, Quatrain 48, he gives the actual end of the world as much later. He writes:

THE THIRD ANTI-CHRIST IS YET TO COME…IN THE YEAR 1999.

The ruins of San Francisco after the tremendous earthquake of 1906 (left). Nostradamus's logic mirrors that of earthquake specialists – that the city will once again be destroyed by earthquakes and fire. It is merely a question of when.

Right: *Perhaps more than any other symbol of our age, the mushroom cloud explosion of an atomic bomb has burned itself into mankind's collective soul.*

Twenty-seven years after the reign of the moon passes, seven thousand years another will hold his monarchy. When the sun shall resume his days past, then is my prophecy accomplished and ended.

Erika Cheetham translates his prophecy thus: 'According to Roussat the cycle of the Moon lasted from 1535–1889, which places the date of the first line as 1555, the publication date of the first part of the Centuries. Nostradamus seems to envisage another 7,000 years from that date to the cycle of the sun when all will be accomplished. It is as though Nostradamus believes the Centuries are written at the start of a new era lasting 7,000 years.'

Even after the third anti-Christ, then, there is still hope for humanity.

VISIONS OF THE FUTURE
Prophets, Psychics and Seers

THE ORACLE OF DELPHI

For 1000 years mankind sought guidance from the gods of Olympus at the shrine of Apollo at Delphi.

O racles are shrines where gods are said to speak with mortals through the mouths of priests – and none is more famous than that of the Pythia of Delphi, a shrine constructed by the ancient Greeks in homage to the god Apollo. Here was the most influential oracle of the classical world, built on the slopes of Mount Parnassus, north of the Gulf of Corinth, where people came to commune with their gods and be guided by their wisdom.

The cult of Apollo spread rapidly throughout the ancient world – he was regarded as the best and brightest of the ancient Greek gods as the deity of music, archery, prophecy, healing and animals, and he was identified with the Sun. Legend has it that Jupiter, seeking dominance over the central point of the Earth, despatched two eagles to fly in opposite directions over the globe and they met at Delphi, which the gods then called the Navel of the Earth. Fumes were seen issuing from a cave near the site, laying the foundations for the idea that the spot was mystical and linked with the gods in Olympus. It acquired its Pythian forename from the legend of Apollo slaying the Python, a snake-like dragon.

The oracle was run by priests who interpreted the incoherent ramblings of the Pythia, a middle-aged woman dressed as a young maiden who sat on a tripod inhaling fumes of chopped herbs and spiced oil. It's not known why a certain woman was chosen, but she became the conduit between the priests and the gods, with citizens of Greece paying for the privilege of learning their fortunes. It lasted for 1000 years: after the Greeks the Romans and even conquerors from the Orient believed in its mystical properties. Socrates, the great philosopher, wrote of the profound changes which overcame pilgrims who journeyed to it.

In the 5th and 4th centuries BC it cost an Athenian two days' wages to ask the oracle questions. Mediums – there was always a minimum of three working a shift system – were on hand to work morning to night on the allotted days that consultations with the gods were allowed. Knowledge seekers made written requests to the Pythia and she went into a trance-like state after inhaling the herb and oil mixture. When the incoherent mutterings spewed forth, they were interpreted by the priests for the customer. Apollo's influence over the ancient Greek world – a world of civility, modera-

Below: The great scholar Homer, seen here meditating upon the Iliad. *He was one of the great chroniclers of the Oracle of Delphi.*

Left: Apollo Killing the Python, *as painted by J.M.W. Turner and displayed in the National Gallery, London. The dragon and the god were both principal players in fortune telling at the oracle.*

tion and conservatism – is regarded by historians as being particularly important. These values were passed on to the pilgrims at Delphi, making the shrine a moral as well as a metaphysical force for its believers. Carved in a pillar of a temple at Delphi are the maxims of the ancients which governed Greece: 'Know thyself', 'Nothing in excess', 'Go surely', and 'Ruin is at hand'.

Historians believe the first seekers of truth at the oracle wanted merely to learn if their hunting would be good the next day or if their crops would ripen. As time went on the oracle assumed an ever-larger role and the direction of the gods was sought in all the affairs of state. Answers were frequently ambiguous – which left them wide open to interpretation but guaranteed that they could never be accused of being wrong!

The summoning of Olympian guidance at Delphi lasted until well into the Christian epoch. Apollo is said to have delivered his last advice in the year AD 362 to the Emperor Julian who sought to restore pagan gods and worship to his Byzantine empire. Julian said that when he sought advice from Apollo the message came

back: 'Tell the king that the curiously built temple has fallen to the ground, that bright Apollo no longer has a roof over his head, or prophetic laurel, or babbling spring. Yes, even the murmuring water has dried up.'

Below: *Socrates, the philosopher, whose humanitarian and scholarly wisdom was embodied in a thousand years of Greek learning.*

ST MALACHY – Predictor of Popes

Right: *Pope Pius V, pontiff from 1566 to 1572. Malachy called him 'The Angel of the Wood' in his amazing prophecies on the popes.*

Nine hundred years ago an Irish monk predicted the line of popes that would lead the Roman Catholic church up to and beyond modern times.

S. PIVS V. Michael Ghisilerius, Alexan: drin? creat? die 7. Ian uarij an.1566. Sed: it an.6. men.3.dies 24. Obijt die i.Ma ij an.1572 .Vac. Sed.dies 12.

Pope Innocent III (below), *one of the greatest medieval figures. His ecclesiastical reforms were far-reaching.*

Using symbolic titles, set down in Latin, Malachy O'Morgair – monk, bishop and later saint of the Catholic Church – bequeathed to the world an

astonishing set of prophecies in which he successfully predicted the succession of Roman pontiffs from Celestine II in 1143 to the present day. A learned scholar, a man of outstanding wisdom, virtue and humanity, his stunning prophecies were not even discovered until 400 years after his death.

He was born in Ireland in 1094, and was given the Gaelic name Mael Maedoc ua Morgair. Ireland was a wild, dark place in those times, the only physical and spiritual havens being the monasteries which dotted her bleak landscape. His father, Mugron, was a professor at Armagh, the country's seat of piety and learning, and from his earliest days Malachy – the name which he adopted when he entered the church – was drawn to Christianity. He studied under the Abbot of Armagh and in 1119 was ordained as a priest. He became Abbot of Bangor in 1123. With this rise in his status he embarked upon clerical reforms.

Ireland's ecclesiastical system was in a state of chaos. The church was still basically a tribal hierarchy, based on the system set up by St Patrick. Paganism was rife in the countryside (mainly due to marauding Danes). The clergy was corrupt, the churches in disrepair, the people left in a state of religious limbo between heresy and Catholicism. Malachy made it his task to reform the church. He was responsible for bringing in the Roman liturgy, Christian marriage rites and the Latin mass.

In 1140 he journeyed to Rome and, *en route*, stopped at a French monastery at Clairvaux, where he befriended Abbot Bernard – later St Bernard – who subsequently wrote a contemporary biography of Malachy's life. So impressed was Malachy with the Cistercian way of living, as practised by Bernard and his brothers, that he requested Pope Innocent II at the Vatican to relieve him of his bishopric to become a simple disciple at Clairvaux. The pope refused, saying that there was much work for him still to do in Ireland. While he was in Rome the pope announced that Malachy was to be papal legate over all Ireland. Returning to his country with renewed vigour, Malachy brought paganism to an end and order to the church.

Malachy was intrigued by mystical theology – as was St Bernard – and he demonstrated some amazing prophetical attributes. One story has it that he was able to foretell what he was to be given to eat on a given day three months hence. He even gave a grim prediction regarding himself: that he would die at Clairvaux on his next visit there. Sure enough, on 2 November 1148 while resting there, *en route* to Rome, he passed away surrounded by the entire community. In 1190 he was canonized by Pope Clement III, and became the first Irish-born saint.

His life was well chronicled by St Bernard, and other essays on his life and times have dealt with his good works and his teachings, but no contemporary mention was ever made of the prophecies. It wasn't until 1559, when the Benedictine historian Anrold Wion mentioned them in his work *Lignum Vitae*, that the world knew of their existence. In 1871 the Abbé Cucherat in France put forward his theory that Malachy had visions between 1139 and 1140 during his first papal visit. He said that he committed these visions to paper and handed the manuscript to Pope Innocent II. Innocent II then placed the manuscript in the archives where they remained undisturbed for four centuries. It is still not entirely clear how they eventually surfaced into the public domain. What is patently clear, however, is

both their appeal and their accuracy.

Malachy did not come straight out and say 'so and so will become pontiff'. Instead he used a practice later made famous by Nostradamus, of wrapping up his visions with quirky Latin and secular images. His phrases were short – no more than four words – but within them, say the interpreters of the prophecies, lay the clues to the papal succession. The first, for instance, he called '*Ex Castro Tiberis*', which translates into 'From a castle on the Tiber'. Guido de Castello (or 'castle') was the first pontiff who ruled from 1143 to 1144. The second he titled '*Inimicus Expulsus*', or 'The enemy expelled' which translated into Lucius II, pontiff from 1144 to 1145. Lucius II was born Gerardo Caccianemici. '*Cacciare*' in Italian means to expel and '*nemici*' are the enemies. In his reign Lucius II suffered severe head injuries as he attempted to expel a foreign army from Rome. The third pontiff was Eugene III, called '*Ex Magnitude Montis*' by Malachy, meaning 'From the great mountain'. His place of birth was Montemagno and he ruled from 1145 to 1153.

The list of the popes as predicted by Malachy, with the descriptions he attached

Above: *Pope Pius XII, formerly Cardinal Eugenio Pacelli, whom Malachy foresaw as 'An angelic shepherd'.*

Above: *Pope John Paul II at the Mass held at Coventry on the third day of his visit to Britain in 1982.*

to each, continues with Anastasius IV, 'Abbot from Suburra' and Adrian IV, 'From a white country'. Adrian IV was born Nicholas Breakspear and was the only English pope to date; England was known as Albion, the white country.

A little research will reveal how Malachy's descriptions link with the popes who followed: Alexander III, 'From the guardian goose'; Victor IV, 'From the loathsome prison'; Paschal Transtiberina, 'The road beyond the Tiber'; Calixtus III, 'From the Hungary of Tuscia'; Lucius III, 'The light at the door'; Urban III, 'A sow in a sieve'; Gregory VIII, 'The sword of Lawrence'; Clement III, 'He shall go forth from the school'; Celestine III, 'From the Bovensian territory'; Innocent III, 'A signed count'; Honorius III, 'A canon from the side'; Gregory IX, 'The bird of Ostia'; Celestine IV, 'The Sabinian lion'; Innocent IV, 'Count Laurence'; Alexander IV, 'The standard of Ostia'; Urban IV, 'Jerusalem of Champagne'; Clement IV, 'The dragon crushed'; Gregory X, 'The man of the serpent'; Innocent V, 'A French preacher';

Adrian V, 'A good count'; John XXI, 'A Tuscan fisherman'; Nicholas III, 'The modest rose'; Martin IV, 'From the office of Martin of the lilies'; Honorius IV, 'From the leonine rose'; Nicholas IV, 'A woodpecker among the food'; Celestine V, 'Elevated from the desert'; Boniface VII, 'From a blessing of the waves'.

For modern times Malachy predicted Pius IX, 'The cross from a cross'; Leo XIII, 'A light in the sky'; Pius X, 'The burning fire'; Benedict XV, 'Religion laid waste' (this is a particularly interesting one – Malachy saw that, indeed, with the coming of this pope in 1914, his reign was overshadowed by the holocaust of World War 1 which destroyed the Christian menfolk of Europe in endless slaughter); Pius XI, 'Unshaken faith'; Pius XII, 'An angelic shepherd'; John XXIII, 'Pastor and mariner'; Paul VI, 'Flower of flowers'.

In 1978 Pope John Paul I, Albino Luciani, was elected. Malachy had given for this Holy Father the clue of 'Of the half Moon'. A half-moon was over the world when he died 33 days later. Later that same year Pope John Paul II was elected, for whom Malachy had written 'From the eclipse of the Sun'. As the 263rd pastor of the Holy Church, students of Malachy believe that this is a reference to Karol Wojtyla's ability to eclipse the work of previous popes, which in his remarkable career he has managed to do.

The next pope listed by Malachy is described as '*Gloria Olivae*', or 'The glory of the olive'. The olive branch has always been associated with peace and Benedictines are also known as the Olivetans, which may well account for this reference. Apart from that it is impossible yet to say who the next pope will be.

Malachy lists the last pope – although he does not specify whether there will be any between 'The glory of the olive' and this one – as *Petrus Romanus*, 'Peter the Roman'. He concludes the prophecies saying: 'In the final persecution of the Holy Roman Church there will reign Peter the Roman, who will feed his flock among many tribulations, after which the seven-hilled city will be destroyed and the dreadful judge will judge the city.' As an omen of what may happen to Rome one day, it is a sombre one.

MOTHER SHIPTON – Prophetess of Tomorrow

While she was in a state of trance, Yorkshirewoman Mother Shipton foresaw the future, and was able to predict all of the major technological developments that were to come.

Mother Shipton was a legendary British prophetess, born in the reign of King Henry VII and credited with foretelling the deaths of Cardinal Wolsey and Lord Percy, as well as painting a remarkable portrait of the shape of things to come in the modern world. Her most famous rhyming couplets depict an H.G. Wells-type world that was remarkable for its accuracy:

Above: *A Punch and Judy show, similar to the ones that travelled all over Britain in the 18th and 19th centuries.*

'Carriages without horses shall go,
And accidents fill the world with woe.
Around the world thoughts shall fly,
In the twinkling of an eye.
The world upsidedown shall be,
And gold be found at the root of a tree.
Through hills man shall ride,
And no horse be at his side.
Under water men shall walk,
Shall ride, shall sleep, shall talk.
In the air men shall be seen,
In white, in black, in green.
Iron in the water shall float,
As easily as a wooden boat.
Gold shall be found and shown,
In a land that's now not known.
Fire and water shall wonders do,
England at last shall admit a foe.
The world to an end shall come,
In eighteen hundred and eighty one.'

It was later learned that the final lines, about the end of the world, were an unscrupulous

A glorious chapter in British history (left): *the victory of the British longbowmen over the French knights at the Battle of Agincourt, 1415.*

Above: *London's burning – the great prophetess Mother Shipton was among the seers who foretold the demise of the medieval capital.*

THE HIDEOUS OLD HAG PREDICTED THE MAJOR TECHNICAL INNOVATIONS OF OUR WORLD TODAY.

Mary, Queen of Scots (**right**), *whose execution on the block was predicted four years in advance by John Dee.*

addition to her premonitions by a publisher hoping to cash in on her fame in a publication of her works in the last century, but in one short poem, Mother Shipton captured all of the major technical innovations that humanity would perfect over the coming years. She spoke of cars – and the accidents they caused – the telegraph system, motorcycles, diving suits and submarines, flying machines, gold in South Africa and the harnessing of energy for humanity's benefit. It was the Victorian bookseller Charles Hindley who, in 1862, published the latter verses in a pamphlet that was itself a reprint of a 1684 booklet entitled *The Life and Death of Mother Shipton.*

The information is sketchy on Mother Shipton – certainly, her life, simple as it was, never achieved the scrutiny of countrymen like John Dee. The wife of a Yorkshire carpenter, born in 1488 at a place known as the Dropping Well, near Knaresborough, Yorkshire, she was baptized Ursula Southell, changing her name when she married Toby Shipton. She was, by all contemporary accounts, an ugly woman. An account written of her prophecies in 1797 describes her thus: 'Her stature was larger than common, her body crooked, her face frightful, but her understanding extraordinary.' A hunchback, by all accounts, some believe that the Punch and Judy shows beloved of British children at seaside resorts and fêtes have Mr Punch modelled on Mother Ship-

ton. However, it is for her prophecies, rather than her physical traits, for which she is best remembered.

Mother Shipton did not conform to any accepted occult or mystical practices for her prophecies. Rather, she went into trance-like states for hours and would wake up to tell friends and family who had been waiting for her predictions what had occurred. In such a manner she successfully foretold the success of King Henry's routing of the French at Agincourt, Cardinal Wolsey's arrest for treason, the Caesarian birth of Edward VI, the reign of a maiden queen – Elizabeth I – and the beheading of a widowed one, Mary, Queen of Scots. She also, like Nostradamus, successfully predicted a 'great fire consuming London'.

In 1641 a pamphlet appeared entitled *The Prophesie of Mother Shipton, in the Raigne of King Henry the Eighth, Foretelling the Death of Cardinal Wolsey, the Lord Percy and Others, As Also What Should Happen in Insuing Times.* Four years later the famous astrologer William Lilly published a collection of *Ancient and Modern Prophecies* which included what he called 'Shipton's Prophecy' of what would happen in the world.

She died in 1561; undoubtedly, had she been more highly born, more of her remarkable life would have been chronicled. As it is, little survives as testimony to her strange powers.

JOHN DEE –
Unscrupulous Rogue or
Brilliant Astrologer?

Tudor scholar John Dee became personal astrologer to Queen Elizabeth I before apparently losing his powers and falling from favour.

Charlatan, rogue and impostor – or brilliant mathematician, astrologer and crystal gazer, true sage and worthy of the praise that his believers heaped on him? Researches into this intriguing man have left the argument unresolved after almost four centuries.

Dee, born in 1527 to a noble Welsh family in Mortlake, received a fine education. At the age of 15 he went to Cambridge University where his zeal for study astounded his contemporaries.

After graduating he plunged into

D. Dee avoucheth his Stone is brought by Angelicall Ministry.

John Dee – the man upon whom Shakespeare is said to have based the character of Prospero. Dee was truly 'connected' to the high and mighty – but the debate about his talents still rages.

Above: *Philip of Spain. He became one of the crowned heads of Europe happy to entertain John Dee and retain his services as a fortune teller.*

Elizabeth I (right), *who appointed Dee 'hyr astrologer' and had a high opinion of his powers.*

astronomy, deciding to pursue the study of the stars in Holland and Belgium. He returned to England with newly devised astronomical instruments, and also with books on magic and the occult.

He began casting horoscopes and was much influenced by Geronimo Cardano, the Italian physician and astrologer. He amassed a vast library of works on astrology and mysticism and was soon commissioned by Queen Mary I to read horoscopes for her and her future husband, Philip of Spain. Through his cousin Blanche Parry, maid of honour to Princess Elizabeth, he came into contact with the future queen. He drew up her horoscope and compared it to that of Mary. Mary, he told her, would die

childless while Elizabeth's own future was a bright one. Unfortunately for him, a spy in her camp sent word of his account to Mary and he was arrested and spent two years in jail on the charge of 'trying to take the life of the monarch through magic'.

Following Elizabeth's accession he was appointed 'hyr astrologer'. His first task was to predict a suitable day for her coronation. He chose 14 January 1559. The weather was fine and sunny – reinforcing the queen's view of his powers.

He travelled extensively abroad, buying massive libraries of occult and astrological works, and greatly increased his scientific and mathematical knowledge. Indeed, he is credited with foreseeing the invention of the telescope by studying the refraction of light, and suggested its military use.

He returned to a house at Mortlake-on-Thames provided for him by the queen. Here he became famous for his astrology and his prophecies. He found the lost basket of clothes of a neighbour after having a prophetic vision in a dream. He also helped a butler locate his master's missing silver in the same way. He began crystal gazing – the practice of staring into the point of light at the centre of a sphere of glass – from which

bounce back telepathically received ideas, hallucinations or images transmitted by supernormal means. However, he had minimal success with gazing and decided to use the services of mediums.

Edward Kelly joined his household as a crystal 'scryer', or reader, at a salary of £20 per year after summoning the angel Uriel to appear in the ball for Dee. Kelly is widely regarded as the person who chiefly devalued the scholarly Dee's reputation with his hocus-pocus and his mystical incantations in which he summoned up the spirits of the dead. But there appears to have been something to him; believers in Dee feel that his interplay with the angels was genuine and that he attained telepathy and spiritualism with a nether-world never previously reached. Dee laboriously wrote down the conversations he had with numerous angels summoned forth by Kelly.

In the margin of one book, four years before she was executed, Dee drew an axe next to the name of Mary Queen of Scots – and got the date of her execution right. He also predicted 'the sea full of ships' after Uriel revealed plans about a foreign power preparing a 'vast fleet against the welfare of England'. Queen Elizabeth was grateful to Dee for warning her of the Spanish Armada.

In 1583 Dee brought Prince Adalbert Laski, representative of the King of Poland, to Mortlake to observe his angel-summoning sessions with Kelly. During one seance an attendant to the prince burst into the room uninvited, much to the displeasure of Dee and Laski. Dee said the angel told him that within five months the boy would be 'devoured by fishes'. Sure enough, five months later, the boy drowned at sea. Laski stayed on in the house searching for the mythical formula which turned base metals into gold before he departed with Dee and Kelly on a six-year odyssey to the Continent. While abroad they earned the patronage of counts and princes, an offer to reside in Moscow from the Russian royal family, and a rebuke from the pope about their 'unchristian' activities.

Elizabeth, missing 'hyr astrologer', consulted him about how to defeat the Spanish Armada which he had foreseen. Her military advisers urged her to attack the Spanish ships while still in foreign ports, but he said a consultation on her horoscope had shown that the Spanish fleet must be

defeated in English waters. The advice was heeded and he returned to England in a splendid coach provided by his monarch, but the relationship with Kelly was shattered over his command that an angel had informed him that Dee was obliged to share his wife with him!

In England, Dee's fortunes rapidly went downhill. His library had been ransacked by a mob during his absence abroad and he was facing poverty. He tried to recapture his earlier successes from the crystal ball, but nothing seemed to work. Eventually, Elizabeth tired of him and in 1595 she gave him the Wardenship of Christ's College in Manchester, a post he held for ten years before he returned to Mortlake, where he died in 1608.

Richard Deacon, who has made an authoritative study of John Dee, said: 'Some writers have depicted him as the foolish dupe of Kelly. Others have suggested that both he and Kelly used crystal gazing to obtain money fraudulently from Laski. But if it was through greed that Dee exploited the crystal then why reject the Czar's magnificent offer?' Deacon thinks that Dee was a spy for Elizabeth, passing back intelligence on his last mission – perhaps bolstered with astrological readings – to her court. He concludes: 'Dee...was a sincere seeker after knowledge, a mystic at heart but a scientist in his mind, and in many respects a pioneer in a variety of scientific fields.'

The destruction of the Spanish Armada (above). *Queen Elizabeth is understood to have obeyed the warning of her seer, who said the fleet must be destroyed in British waters.*

THE ANGEL HAD INSTRUCTED DEE TO SHARE HIS WIFE WITH KELLY.

CAGLIOSTRO – Prince of Quacks?

Showman or seer, charlatan or sage? Historians once differed immensely on the qualities of Count Alessandro Cagliostro (right), but now he is recognized as a genuine seeker after truth.

> 'IN SPITE OF POSSESSING ALL THE CHARACTERISTICS OF A CHARLATAN, HE NEVER BEHAVED AS SUCH.'

Below: A brutal and enduring symbol of the French Revolution. Madame Guillotine was never unemployed during the dark days of 'the Terror' which followed the overthrow of the House of Bourbon.

Famed in France as the 'Divine Cagliostro', this versatile count conducted experiments in a search for the key to the secrets of the Universe.

Sometimes branded a showman – and cruelly dubbed a 'Prince of Quacks' by Thomas Carlyle – Count Alessandro Cagliostro was an enthusiast of the occult and the mysterious. He was a genuine seeker after knowledge, who strived to unravel the 'heavenly magic' which he believed held the key to the secrets of the Universe.

Little is known of his early life and education. He arrived in London in 1776 with his young wife, Sarafina, whereupon he made contact with Freemasons' groups intent on turning base metals into gold. He held seances, summoned up spirits, and on three occasions at least predicted the winning numbers of a lottery. His main interest, however, was divining the affinity between the Church, Freemasonry and other religions.

His first supernatural experiments are chronicled as having taken place in 1779. Using an Egyptian method of clairvoyancy he had discovered, he hypnotized a child, causing him to see visions and utter prophecies. As the subject was induced into a trance-like state, Cagliostro strove for his 'heavenly magic' by summoning angels to speak for him with God.

In one Egyptian rite ceremony Cagliostro employed the nephew of the Countess Elsa von der Recke. Cagliostro had earlier asked the husband of the Countess what sort of vision he would wish the boy to have. He suggested it be of his mother and sister who were some kilometres away in another village. Ten minutes later the boy – having no idea who he would see under Cagliostro's 'spell' – cried out that he saw his mother and sister, and that his sister was holding her 'hand to her heart as if in pain'.

Cagliostro later sent an emissary to check on the family. It was discovered that the sister had recently suffered such violent heart palpitations that she thought she was dying! It is worth pointing out that Cagliostro was privately wealthy and never charged money for any of these seances.

Soon afterwards he moved across France, before arriving in Paris where he was lauded as the 'Divine Cagliostro'. Here, fresh from his successes, he assumed the role of a master magician and held many seances in which phantoms and angels were invoked in glass vases of water. This led to an introduction to King Louis XVI where he performed the same spectacular feats at Versailles.

Cagliostro also possessed seemingly remarkable powers of healing. There exist numerous accounts of the potions and elixirs which he dispensed to the sick. He was also one of the earliest believers in the powers of crystal healing. With his massive library of books, which included pharmaceutical and herbalist works, it is likely that many of his potions were used in tandem with the crystals. And again, he refused all payment for his services.

Cagliostro moved on to prophecies. At a masonic meeting held at the home of a noted occultist he expounded the theory of Gematria – that all letters of the alphabet

have a numerical value and that a person's future could be foretold from the total of the digits his or her name represented. For the king he forecast a violent end to his life as he neared 39; for the queen, Marie Antoinette, he said she would become 'prematurely wrinkled through sorrow', would languish in prison and then would be beheaded on the scaffold. For her close companion, the Princess de Lamballe, he said she would die on the corner of the street named Rue des Ballets. ALL of these predictions turned out frighteningly true.

And there was more – he predicted that a Corsican would end the Revolution and that his name would be Napoleon Bonaparte. Although a victorious general at first, Cagliostro said Napoleon would finish his days 'pacing the circle of a melancholy island' – an accurate reference to his exile to Elba.

Cagliostro's downfall came when he was falsely accused of stealing a necklace worth hundreds of thousands of francs. He spent nine months in the notorious Bastille before being found not guilty in a trial which inflamed the passions of the poor against the nobility, and upon his acquittal he was ordered to leave France by the king himself. It was 1786, three years before the French Revolution would sweep away Europe's old orders forever. He returned with his wife to England where he published a pamphlet predicting the Revolution, the storming of the hated Bastille gaol, and the downfall of the French monarchy.

Seeking fulfilment and peace elsewhere,

Above: *Napoleon at the Battle of Wagram, July 1809. Cagliostro prophesied his coming, marking him down as the man who would end the Revolution.*

Left: *Louis XVI, king of France from 1754 to 1793, granted permission for Cagliostro to summon up the spirits of dead ancestors – in the great Hall of Mirrors at the Versailles palace!*

Right: *This mosaic was found at Pompeii in 1874. It includes a number of symbols of a secret society akin to Freemasonry.*

HE WAS SUBJECTED TO HORRIFIC TORTURES BUT HE REFUSED TO DENY THE TRUTH OF HIS PREDICTIONS.

The storming of the Bastille (below), hated symbol of monarchist rule. It was liberated by the mob.

the couple moved to Rome. Here, freemasonry was banned but Cagliostro wanted to recapture his fame and fortune. He held one illegal seance with some Rome noblemen before he was arrested. At the seance in 1789 he used a young girl as the conduit with the spirit world. She uttered words about a mob armed with sticks, racing towards a place called Versailles: she had accurately predicted the start of the Revolution which did not take place for a further three weeks. The French ambassador, the Cardinal de Bernis, was among those present at the seance; he was outraged at the prediction that his lord and master was about to be destroyed. 'I am sorry, my Lord Cardinal,' said Cagliostro. 'But the prophecy will be realized.'

The vengeful ambassador told the Inquisition about him and Cagliostro was placed under close supervision before being arrested on 27 December 1789. He endured horrific tortures before being tried and found guilty of heresy, sorcery and Freemasonry. The pope commuted his sentence to life imprisonment, the same fate prescribed for his wife. She died in captivity in 1794, he a year later following a fit. Had he lived for two more years the French, under the warrior Napoleon whom he foresaw, would have liberated him.

CHEIRO – Prophet of the Politicians

From an early age Cheiro had astounding powers of prediction. Later he travelled widely and was consulted by the world's leaders.

Cheiro, born William John Warner, is probably the most successful of clairvoyants from the last century.

Born on 1 November 1866, he found himself at an early age blessed with strange gifts. He found he could easily read the palms of his classmates and teachers. Later, after his father was ruined by a disastrous land deal – as Cheiro had foretold – he read the palm of a stranger on a train. He told the man he was another Napoleon, with a great destiny, but that he would meet his own 'Waterloos' in the shape of a beautiful woman. Years later the man, Charles Stuart Parnell, was brought down in the divorce of Katherine O'Shea.

Cheiro travelled to India, where he delved into transcendental meditation and out-of-body experience. He stayed for three years before inheriting a fortune from a relative, and then returned to London.

One of his successes was in helping to solve a murder in the East End. Police called upon him to 'read' a bloodstained palmprint left on a door jamb at the scene of the killing. Cheiro said that the palmprint was that of the murdered man's illegitimate son, whose existence was not known at that stage by the police. Three weeks later the son was arrested and charged with the murder. Cheiro soon became bored with London and took himself off to the temples of the Nile where he acquired the severed hand of a mummified princess. The hand travelled with him constantly after he returned to London to try to become a full-time teacher of occult studies. The name Cheiro, from the Greek word *cheir* for hand, came to him in a premonition and he became permanently known by it.

Arthur James Balfour, later the Tory prime minister, was one of his first clients, and he brought along with him a wealthy and fashionable clientele, but fortune telling, as defined by law, was illegal under laws dating back to Henry VIII. Police warned him to cease his practice within a week or face prosecution, but thanks to influential friends he managed to keep going. He went on to read the palms of several members of the nobility. A famous reading occurred in the home of a friend, Blanche Roosevelt, who insisted on him reading the hands of someone through a curtain. He said: 'The left hand is the hand of a king, but the right that of a king who will send himself into exile.' The owner of the hand asked when, and was told, 'A few

---

HE 'READ' THE BLOODSTAINED PALMPRINT AND IDENTIFIED THE MURDERER.

Oscar Wilde (below). *The dandy wit and playwright had his hand read by Cheiro without revealing his identity. Cheiro foretold that he had the hand of a man 'destined to send himself into exile'. Wilde ended up in Reading gaol.*

Above: Czar Nicholas Romanov and his son Alexis in 1911 – six years before the Revolution which would sweep away their dynasty's rule of all the Russias.

Arthur Balfour (above right), in a photograph by W.D. Downey, was a patron of Cheiro, and he brought to this remarkable man a wealthy and élite clientele.

years from now, at about your fortieth year.' Cheiro later learned he had foretold the future for Oscar Wilde.

Cheiro moved to the USA in 1894 and became an instant hit after reading the palmprints of several prominent Americans. One of them was of a man who had recently been arrested for murder. Without knowing the man, a Dr Meyer of Chicago who was poisoning his patients with potions, Cheiro predicted that he would die peacefully in prison after many years behind bars. On the eve of his execution Cheiro again read his hand – and said that he would be reprieved. The next day the Supreme Court commuted his sentence to life imprisonment. He died in jail 15 years later.

Another stunningly accurate prediction was to a Mrs Leiter of Chicago who gave him a print of her daughter's hand. He prophesied that the girl would marry a man from another country and then 'lead the life

of a queen in the East, but she will die young'. Mary Leiter became Lord Curzon's wife and later Vicereine of India. Tragically she died young.

Cheiro spoke all over the USA, saying that a baby an hour old has lines on its hands that foretell its future. Eventually, richer but bored, he returned to England, fed up with the questions from clients that mostly demanded to know how they could be richer and when it would happen.

Even King Edward VII consulted Cheiro at the Belgrave Square house of an American society friend. At the reading Cheiro told the king that the numbers six and nine would be the most significant in his life. He died in his 69th year. Cheiro also accurately foretold the month the king's coronation would take place: August 1902.

King Leopold II of the Belgians was another client who consulted Cheiro – but the news was grim. Cheiro said the king's death in 1909 would be caused by serious problems with his digestive tract. He died on 17 December that year, the cause of death given as 'the complete breakdown of the digestive organs and intestinal obstruction'. Another reading for the Czar of Russia was foreboding but true: 'He will be haunted by the horrors of war and bloodshed…his name will be bound up with some of the most far reaching and bloodiest wars in history, and in the end, about 1917, he will lose all he loves most by sword or strife in one form or another, and he himself will meet a violent death.' Cheiro had predicted the end of the Romanov dynasty and the Russian Revolution.

Georgi Rasputin, the evil monk who held so much sway over the czarina, was also a client. Cheiro told him that he would be a power for evil, holding enormous sway over others. He told him he would die by bullets and would finally be dumped in the Neva River – exactly, as it turned out, how Rasputin did meet his end.

Herbert Kitchener, the great Lord Kitchener of Sudan, consulted him on 21 July 1894 at the War Office. Cheiro said he would be in great danger in 1916, caused by a storm at sea. Kitchener died that year on board a vessel bound for Russia that struck a mine.

Cheiro went on to predict the election result for a Conservative MP in a marginal seat, the Wall Street Crash of 1929 for a businessman and saved the Shah of Persia

from an assassination attempt. He did not, however, manage to predict the crash of his own fortunes, which came when he made a disastrous business deal involving the purchase of an American newspaper.

After World War 1 Cheiro foretold the treaty in 1926 between Soviet Russia and Germany, the General Strike in Britain in May 1926, the breaking out of civil war in China and an earthquake in the Channel Islands. All came true. In 1927 he published a book of world predictions, stunning in their accuracy. He foretold the return of the Jews to Palestine in a state they would call Israel, World War 2 and the spread of communism throughout the world. In 1930 he went to live in Hollywood with the intention of becoming a scriptwriter, but he wrote only one screenplay – about Cagliostro – and it was never made. He ran his own school of metaphysics there until his death in 1936.

HIS TRAGIC PREDICTIONS HAD AN UNFORTUNATE KNACK OF COMING TRUE.

Left: *Lord Kitchener, chief of the general staff at the outbreak of World War 1. He consulted Cheiro, who told him he would be in great danger in 1916. That year he died at sea en route to Russia.*

WOLF MESSING –
Stalin's Psychic

A Polish Jew had such powers of mental gymnastics that he acquired the patronage of no less a person than Josef Stalin.

Josef Stalin, history's bloodiest dictator, at one time placed his faith in Wolf Messing, who was undoubtedly Russia's greatest-ever seer. Messing, who discovered his gifts as an 11-year-old boy, is regarded by many as one of the great psychics of this century.

Born a Polish Jew near Warsaw on 10 September 1899 Messing was a subject then of Imperial Russia and its last czar, Nicholas II. He ran away from school when he was 11 and boarded a train for Berlin with no ticket. He was caught by a brutal ticket collector who asked him repeatedly for his ticket; Messing ended up handing him a scrap of paper from his pocket – and thereby performed his first conscious act of mental gymnastics. He recalled: 'Our gazes crossed. How I desperately wanted him to accept that scrap of paper as a ticket!... I mentally suggested to him: "It is a ticket... it is a ticket...it is a ticket..." The iron jaws of the ticket punch snapped. Handing the "ticket" back to me and smiling benevolently he asked me why I had been sleeping under the seat when I had a valid ticket. It was the first time my power of suggestion manifested itself.'

After suffering grinding poverty and chronic malnutrition in Berlin, Messing gradually managed to carve himself a living as a mind-reader in city theatres. By placing himself into a light trance he found he could concentrate on the thoughts uppermost in a person's mind. He earned the grand sum of five marks a day.

Right: *The Kremlin in Moscow. It was here that Stalin put the unique talents of Wolf Messing to the test.*

Soon his mind-reading abilities brought him into the orbit of the truly great men of his day – Albert Einstein and Sigmund Freud. There is a famous story of how Freud told Einstein that he would 'think' a command for Messing to interpret. On a given day all three were seated in Freud's Vienna salon and Messing, now 17, went into a trance. Soon, he sat upright, walked across to a pair of scissors lying on a desktop, picked them up and proceeded to clip three hairs from Einstein's moustache. Messing had interpreted the mental orders with absolute precision.

Messing toured South America and the Far East during World War 1 and returned to his birthplace, now in an independent Poland, in 1922. After compulsory military service he took up travelling throughout Europe, again performing his mind-reading stunts to amazed audiences. One of his most appreciated performances was the ability to drive a car while totally blindfolded as he received telepathic instructions from a chauffeur about directions.

It was with the coming of Hitler and World War 2 that Messing fled to Moscow – even though the racial policies of Stalin were often just as harsh as those of Hitler. In 1939 he found himself in a squalid apartment in the capital – and in a quandary about how to make a living.

Stalin had banned those who practised extra-sensory perception and other psychic arts, his paranoia leading him to distrust anyone with powers he could not understand. Messing did obtain work as the last act in various nightclubs but on more than one occasion found himself as a guest of the police or the KGB for a night.

Finally, one night, after he was arrested at a club in the town of Gomel, he was presented to someone of 'immense authority'. That person was Stalin himself, and at the meeting he was cordial, asking Messing questions about his life in Poland and the situation there. A few days later Messing was collected by the KGB and subjected to a special test, on Stalin's orders, of his abilities. The 'test' consisted of asking an official of the state bank to hand over 100,000 roubles, presenting him with a piece of blank paper at the same time. Messing said: 'It was essentially a re-run of the test I had on the train.'

There followed several audiences with Stalin in which Messing spoke of his foreboding that Hitler planned war on the

Left: Sigmund Freud – the man who, more than any other, came close to unlocking the secrets of the mind.

BY CONCENTRATING DEEPLY HE COULD READ ANYBODY'S MIND – EVEN THE MURDEROUS STALIN'S.

Below: Josef Stalin, the Kremlin overlord who liked to test Wolf Messing's abilities. More attention to Messing might have shortened the war and saved untold thousands of lives.

Above: *Adolf Hitler. The Messianic leader of Nazi Germany had a closet interest in the occult – but Wolf Messing delivered warnings about him to his arch-enemy Stalin.*

Right: *Wolf Messing, psychic extraordinaire, shown here in the 1950s giving one of his stage shows in Russia. He was a man of quite astonishing powers.*

USSR. Messing told Stalin that he had had a vision that war would come in June 1941. On 22 June that year the full weight of Hitler's mechanized armies fell against the USSR.

During the war years Messing was allowed by Stalin to perform his mind-reading feats in morale-raising public appearances. Later that year he was summoned to the Kremlin where Stalin asked for a personal display of his powers. He recalled: 'He said he did not think anybody could make a fool of him and that I would not be able to leave the Kremlin without a pass signed by him... He telephoned the guards to say I could not leave without a pass and ordered his private secretary to follow ten paces behind me.

'I entered my deepest state of trance that I can ever recall. Several minutes later, I walked right out on to the street past the guards, who remained standing at attention and looking up at the window of Stalin's study. "Maybe I should blow him a kiss," I thought mockingly.'

Stalin looked upon Messing as his personal seer, and he was forever inviting him to his private apartments in the Kremlin. But the 'Man of Steel' did not heed his advice on the war. Stalin seems to have regarded him more as a personal pet, but it was a powerful patronage and one that Messing was keen to engender for as long as possible.

In the 1950s Messing underwent extensive testing at the hands of Soviet scientists, on Stalin's orders, to probe the workings of his extraordinary mind. Until then belief in the paranormal was attacked in Soviet society as being 'bourgeois, materialistic and pseudoscientific' but with Messing they decided that electrical impulses in the brain were acting as radar signals which he bounced off similar strong thought patterns from individuals whose minds he endeavoured to read. Messing was less scientific and said: 'All I know is that I was born with this gift and have always been able to utilise it.'

In his later years Messing toured the USSR, deriving most pleasure from performances of his powers in small villages, where he also gained a reputation as a faith healer. In the early 1970s his health began to fade and he died from a heart attack in 1972, by which time his fame was so widespread within the USSR that he was accorded a hero's burial.

KARL ERNEST KRAFFT
and the Hitler Horoscopes

At first at risk of harassment by the Nazis, Krafft attracted the attention of the leaders of the Third Reich by predicting an attempt on the life of Hitler.

Many dark forces shaped and defined the Third Reich during its 12 years. But lurking in the background was a little-known astrologer called Karl Ernest Krafft. Historians now believe that if Hitler had listened to Krafft more closely, the final outcome of the war might have been very different indeed.

Born in 1900 in Basle, Krafft was a brilliant young man with a genuine gift for figures and statistics, but his greatest love was the study of the planets and astrology. After graduating from university in mathematics, for the best part of ten years he worked on a massive book entitled *Traits of Astro-Biology*. This expounded his own theory of 'Typocosmy' – the prediction of the future based on the study of an individual's personality, or type. By the early 1930s, when Hitler had come to power, Krafft enjoyed a unique status among occultists and prophets in Germany. But ironically, it was the Nazis – later to become his greatest patrons – who at first posed the biggest threat to him. Occultists, like Freemasons, were among those harassed and vilified by the Nazis.

However, while publicly the state may have persecuted astrologers, privately men like Hitler, his right-hand-man Rudolf Hess and the SS chief Himmler were all in favour of consulting them. Krafft moved directly into the orbit of the higher echelons of the Nazi élite in November

1939 when he made a remarkable prediction. He predicted that the Führer's life would be in danger between 7 and 10 November. He wrote, on 2 November, to a friend called Dr Heinrich Fesel who worked for Himmler, warning him of an attempt on Hitler's life. Fesel filed the letter away, unwilling to become enmeshed in something which he felt could become extremely dangerous.

On 8 November, a bomb exploded at a Munich beer hall. There were many injuries, but the man who was targeted, Adolf Hitler, was unscathed. When newspapers reported the near-catastrophe

Deputy Führer Rudolf Hess (centre) was an occult enthusiast. When he flew to Scotland the times became harder for Nazi seers like Karl Ernest Krafft.

Above: *Joseph Goebbels, supreme propagandist of the Third Reich, liked to twist the prophecies of Nostradamus and others into showing Nazism in a favourable light.*

Fesel despatched a telegram to Hess, drawing attention to Krafft's prediction. Krafft was instantly arrested and brought to Gestapo headquarters in Berlin for questioning. Questioning soon proved that he was innocent as far as the attempt on Hitler's life went. After his release he was summoned to the offices of the Reich propaganda ministry, run by Josef Goebbels. Goebbels had recently taken to poring over the historic prophecies of Nostradamus, trying to squeeze from them the maximum amount of propaganda to portray the Third Reich in flattering tones. Krafft, he felt, had the weight and authority to begin work on deciphering the often cryptic quatrains. In January 1940 the Swiss astrologer began work on a pro-German evaluation of Nostradamus.

Krafft was convinced that the prophecies of Nostradamus boded well for the Third Reich. Tens of thousands of pamphlets based upon his interpretations of the quatrains were circulated in various languages and he soon came to the attention of the Führer. In the spring of 1940 he gave a private horoscope reading for Hitler to an

aide, but he never met his leader. Later he boasted to friends that he mentioned that the time for an attack on the USSR was some way off. Hitler, who was impatient to launch Operation Barbarossa (the conquest of the USSR) after he had dealt with the West, in fact delayed his operations in the east until the following June. The stunning success of the early days of Barbarossa convinced him that Krafft had great powers.

British intelligence became so concerned at the thought that their opponent's war was being conducted by a mystic that they, for a time, hired the services of the astrologer Louis De Wohl to divine the kind of prophecies that Krafft was divining for the Nazis. De Wohl was quietly dropped after several months, having failed to procure any hard evidence about Krafft's work.

Krafft warned the Reich leaders that for victory to be certain, the war MUST end for Germany in 1943; in this, it turned out, he was entirely correct. By the end of 1942 Germany was at the zenith of her victories, but after that date the full might of the allies, with the USA behind them, could not fail to eventually swamp the Fatherland.

Left: *Rommel, the Desert Fox. When Krafft was shown astrological charts of both him and Montgomery he declared the British field marshal to be made of stronger stuff.*

IF HITLER HAD TAKEN KRAFFT'S ADVICE, HE MIGHT HAVE WON THE WAR.

Below: *Montgomery of Alamein, who truly did have the mettle, in the end, to take on Rommel and drive him all the way out of Africa.*

Krafft's star was still in the Nazi ascendancy when Rudolf Hess made his astonishing flight to Scotland in 1941. Hitler was outraged. He knew that Hess was the biggest occult supporter of them all and, in his fury, ordered a massive purge of astrologers, occultists and other sages. Even Krafft was caught up in this and he languished in prison for a year before being released. This time he was sent to work on horoscopes of allied generals and admirals. One of his predictions when seeing the charts of both Rommel and Montgomery, adversaries in the desert war, was: 'Well, this man Montgomery's chart is certainly stronger than Rommel's.' History proved him to be correct.

Krafft's health began to fail and he developed a persecution complex. He wrote to a senior official predicting that British bombs would very soon destroy the propaganda ministry in Berlin – another true statement. The letter was passed on to the Gestapo who viewed it as treasonous. He was incarcerated in foul conditions, contracted typhus and eventually died on 8 January 1945.

JOAN QUIGLEY – the Power behind the President

For six years socialite and astrologer Joan Quigley played a major part in world events.

When the story first broke about Joan Quigley's involvement with the Reagan administration in the White House, the impact was shattering. If what was being alleged was true, then for close to six of the eight years that Ronald Reagan ruled as the world's most powerful man his destiny – and therefore humanity's – was linked to Quigley's interpretations of the Universe in her role as an astrologer. Not since medieval times has a soothsayer had so much influence in power-politics.

Below: Joan Quigley. The world was shocked to learn of her star-gazing in the White House, which subjugated the most powerful man in the world to the will of the cosmos.

Quigley was an educated, soft-spoken spinster who lived on San Francisco's luxurious Nob Hill and was considered a major player on the city's social scene. But what drove her was her love for, and her gift of, interpreting the stars.

Plotting future events by the alignment of the heavens was at first an escape for Joan, and then something of a permanent challenge. In the late 1960s and early 1970s she began reading the horoscopes of wealthy Republican friends.

She was introduced to the Reagans in 1973 and soon Nancy Reagan was calling her up on a regular basis. Quigley claimed: 'From 1973 on I drew up horoscopes for both the then governor and Mrs Reagan annually. When I first saw Ronald's horoscope I knew it was world class.'

Reagan became the single most powerful individual on earth with his triumph at the polls in 1980. His rule would lay the foundations for the most cataclysmic changes in world history since the end of the war and herald the beginning of the end for the USA's old arch-enemy, the USSR. During Reagan's first 15 months in office Joan Quigley had little influence, but after he miraculously survived an assassination attempt in March 1981, she became a force to be reckoned with within the corridors of power. For a fee of 3000 US dollars a month she would soon be running the affairs of a superpower – or if not running them, certainly having a major say in them.

Later Joan would recall: 'Nancy was interested in everything, not just the president's safety. She was interested in her image. She wanted me to improve it.' In effect, Quigley became an ex-officio cabinet member. In regular telephone conversations, Quigley would hammer out every nuance of the president's schedule. Nancy became obsessed with working out when would be the most propitious time for him to undertake any aspect of his job. By her own horoscope proved conclusively that he needed an operation for cancer. The doctors that day found out and wanted to operate immediately, but she told Nancy that an operation wouldn't be successful until noon on the 13th. Nancy obeyed her and Reagan did not need further cancer surgery during his entire time in office. But Quigley said: 'Had they not listened to me they would have risked not removing the cancerous growth completely.'

• Staging the announcement in Washington of a controversial Supreme Court Justice. Right-winger Anthony Kennedy's election was not a popular one with moderates and liberals, so Quigley says she used a unique astrological device to pick the exact right time for Reagan to announce his choice. Nancy, she says, went along with her advice and Anthony Kennedy was later installed without fuss or rancour.

• Smoothing over the fuss about Irangate. She claims that between January and August

Nancy Reagan (left), forceful wife of President Reagan. It was at her insistence that astrological charts dominated many aspects of his presidency.

admission Quigley was a powerful force: 'For over seven years I was responsible for timing all press conferences, most speeches, the State of the Union addresses, the take-offs and landings of Air Force One. I picked the times of Reagan's debates with Carter and Mondale and all of his trips. I delayed the president's cancer operation and chose the time for Nancy's mastectomy.' Using what she calls 'analysis' on the data provided by astronomers, and charts calculated by computers, here's what Quigley also takes credit for:

• Overturning Nancy's initial hostility to Gorbachev. Quigley says her examination of Gorbachev's horoscope proved to her that his Aquarian planet sign was in such harmony with Reagan's that they would share a 'beautiful vision'. Quigley credits herself with forcing Reagan to drop his 'evil empire' rhetoric against the Soviet leader.

• Defusing the crisis over the visit by the Reagans to a cemetery in the German town of Bitburg in May 1985 that contained the graves of Nazi SS officers. She completely threw the scheduling into disarray by saying that the planets were only favourable for a visit at 2.45 pm instead of two hours earlier as planned. 'The Bitburg visit was brief,' she said. 'And the controversy soon died down. I defused it for him.'

• Foreseeing also in 1985 the president's need for surgery. She says that on 10 July his

1987, when the scandal about the arms-dealing-for-hostages was at its zenith, she re-organized Reagan's schedule to make it 'practically impossible' for hostile media representatives to get to the president with embarrassing questions.

• Securing the president's safety while

Above: Ronald Reagan, 40th president of the United States and the first ever to have his daily schedule worked out around the signs of the horoscope.

Above: *Mikhail Gorbachev – another world leader with whom Ronald Reagan had a great many dealings. He couldn't have known that his capitalist counterpart was running the White House according to the stars!*

Libyan dictator Colonel Ghaddafi (right). Quigley claims that she advised on the most auspicious time for the US to attack the desert despot in 1986.

airborne. She says that many times she contacted Nancy while Air Force One was transporting President Reagan around the world, dictating flying patterns and landing and take-off times. She remains convinced that his life could have been in jeopardy if her advice had not been heeded.

• Advising him on the most momentous single act of his presidency – the bombing of Libya because of Colonel Gaddafi's continued sponsorship of world terrorists.

Quigley's interpretation of the pageantry of the zodiac may have been vital to Nancy, and even to the president, but it was viewed by professionals within the White House as calamitous. Donald Regan, the chief-of-staff who blew the whistle on the entire affair in 1990, says her stargazing created a hammerlock on business. On his desk he was forced to keep a colour-coded calendar to chart the president's 'good', 'bad' and 'iffy' days and on at least one occasion she gave him a list in which large chunks of time were marked 'stay home' or 'be careful'. Regan claims Quigley chose the most auspicious time for the Aquarian Ronald to meet the Piscean Gorbachev.

'I wanted secrecy more than Nancy,' she said. 'That's why I stayed so much in the background.' However, Regan's book about the stargazing years set the media hounds on the trail and Quigley claims she was forced to go public to protect her own reputation. It caused a rift with Nancy Reagan, but she says she could not lie, not even for the former First Lady.

Quigley also takes the credit for what she calls 'PR by astrology' – smoothing the image of the 'great communicator' and his sometimes frosty wife, but perhaps her greatest claim of all is that she kept Reagan ALIVE. She points out: 'From William Henry Washington on, every president elected in a zero year has died in office except for Reagan. I think I had something to do with that. In fact, I know I did.'

After she no longer worked for Reagan she was so upset about the rift with Nancy that she pledged never, ever to read the horoscopes of an American again.

After she quit working for the Reagans she tried to drop back out of the public limelight, although occasionally she would offer up some predictions on public figures whose horoscopes she was already acquainted with. A year before the abortive August coup in Moscow by hardliners she said this about Gorbachev: 'He's going to have more troubles from his generals and more food shortages. There is going to be a loss of power for him.'

Quigley hasn't made any dramatic predictions for the end of the century in seven years' time. She does, however, offer up one Hollywood prophecy: that volatile couple Ryan O'Neal and Farrah Fawcett might not be together by the year 1999.

J.Z. KNIGHT AND JACK PURSEL – Channellers of Wisdom

Thousands of her supporters follow the teachings of Seattle housewife J.Z. Knight, who claims to be the channel for a warrior from ancient Atlantis.

In a remote mountain ranch in Washington State the faithful adherents of 'channelling' gather like pilgrims every weekend for £500-per-time mind-sessions with the most famous channeller of them all. Judy Z. Knight was a Seattle housewife until she was visited in 1977 by the spirit of a long-dead warrior from the long-lost continent of Atlantis. His name was Ramtha and ever since he has been sending his prophecies and his wisdom to numerous believers – among them *Dynasty* star Linda Evans and Hollywood legend Shirley MacLaine.

The concept of channellers is as old as the centuries – only the term is relatively new. It describes practitioners of prophecies who turn over control of their bodies to spirits of the dead, or to extra-terrestrial beings, who in turn proffer their wisdom, coupled with portents of things to come. J.Z., as she is known to her devotees, has become wealthy and influential through her connection to Ramtha – a Cro-Magnon man, 35,000 years old. The channelling movement offers an exotic way towards spiritual fulfilment and Ramtha is credited by thousands of people as having totally changed their way of living. His 'teachings' seem to consist of bits and pieces of Buddhism, Hinduism and Christianity.

'Ramtha helped me find happiness,' said Hollywood celebrity Linda Evans. 'For me, he has been a powerful teacher. And J.Z. is one psychic who has certainly changed my life.'

Evans first heard Ramtha speak through J.Z. Knight in 1985. She took a day off from the set of soap opera *Dynasty* and drove to a Ramtha seminar near Los Angeles. She said, 'I had been exploring psychic phenomena for close to 20 years, but when I first heard his voice speak I felt it was adding wonderful bridges that I had never come across.

'In the beginning I was totally suspicious. I wanted proof that the channelling wasn't just trickery. I wanted to protect myself. I didn't want to be misled after all I had been through in my personal

Below: *J.Z. Knight – rich, successful and powerful, thanks to her 'channelling' with the spirit of a long-dead warrior from the lost kingdom of Atlantis.*

Right: Seattle housewife J.Z. Knight, channeller of the ancient Atlantean Ramtha.

life. But he holds you in the moment – holds a truth or emotion until you can totally feel and know it. He puts the information in front of you to see. He made me see first off that I could no longer put all the blame on my husband John Derek for leaving me. I had to take responsibility for my part.'

Why did Ramtha decide to impart his knowledge to a Seattle housewife? J.Z. – married five times and recently involved in a messy divorce – said: 'I have no idea why he chose me. I am the medium for him. He speaks and the words come out of my body, but it is not me speaking. It is his voice. When it happened I had mixed feelings. I knew that there would be days that would not belong to me any more. I am his tool. But I have learned so much wisdom from him, which others have too, that I never regret that day.'

Just what does Ramtha offer, other than self-enlightenment, contentment and advice for people to look inside themselves for the clues to the secret of the Universe? At any given session, channelling disciples will ask many wide-ranging, worldly questions – and Ramtha always gives an answer. A man at a seminar in 1990 asked what the best investment for his cash was. Ramtha told him to buy Taiwanese dollars (at the time, a sound investment bet). He predicted the San Francisco earthquake of 1989 and takes credit – through J.Z., of course – for predicting the worldwide recession of 1992. Literally thousands of people have taken the advice of his central philosophy for the 20th century – that people must abandon the cities for a more rural life. That rural life for many is in the surrounding countryside near to J.Z. Knight's home where Ramtha instructs them to 'keep to high ground' and store up to two years' food supplies in the basement for the coming unspecified catastrophe.

Shirley MacLaine is another big-name celebrity who has consulted with Ramtha on numerous occasions as part of her quest for 'new age enlightenment'. She insists that Ramtha is the summoning of a powerful, relevant force that needs to be listened to and reckoned with. MacLaine, who believes she has been, at various times

Shirley MacLaine (below), one of a long line of celebrity clients who have given channelling respectability and status in the US.

in the past, a Peruvian Inca child, a Mongolian maiden and an Indian princess, says that Ramtha has provided her with many valuable lessons.

'I just knew he had been my sibling in a previous existence in Atlantis,' said Mac-Laine. 'He was profound.' Profound, too, is the acceptance that Knight has gained with her ancient guru from among both sceptics and students of the paranormal in the USA. Although at times the media have portrayed Knight as everything from wily cult leader to harmless psychotic to dangerous manipulator, those who have examined Ramtha's teachings find that, for the most part, his wisdom is sound and his predictions true. Arthur Hastings, who studied dozens of channellers for his book *With the Tongues of Man and Angels*, said: 'I am deeply impressed.' Even Charles Tart, author of *Open Mind, Discriminating Mind*, who questions the value of channellers, agrees: 'No high-minded entity, including Ramtha, has ever come up with a carburettor design that would help improve gas mileage, something that would concretely help civilisation. Still, much of what he says makes good common sense.'

If J.Z. Knight is the most famous, and richest, channeller, Jack Pursel from Palm Beach, Florida, runs her a close second with a celebrity client list every bit as good. He summons up Lazaris, a disembodied spirit – not a warrior-god like Ramtha – who calls himself 'the consummate friend'. Lazaris appears to channel his thoughts and predictions through former insurance adjuster Pursel, who quit his climb up the corporate ladder after being visited by the un-incarnate spirit six years ago. Celebrities Sharon Gless, Michael York, Barry Manilow and Lesley Ann Warren – all have credited Lazaris with helping them.

Gless, who won an Emmy award for her role as a New York cop in the *Cagney and Lacey* show, even thanked Lazaris in her acceptance speech when she received the award! Like Ramtha, he works on the basis of inner love and a re-evaluation of the Universe to improve life and health, rather than specific predictions. But at seminars, almost identical to those held by Knight, Lazaris is summoned to speak where he offers wisdom on such practical matters as health care and finances. One woman suffering from pancreatic cancer credits him with saving her life after telling her to recuperate in a yellow room. Another, a man, claimed Lazaris accurately predicted a fall in certain share prices.

Like Knight, Pursel can give no reason why this force in the spirit world should have chosen to visit him. He added: 'If we can add to the sum total of knowledge, though, in the world, and its happiness, surely that can't be a bad thing, can it? He has a great deal of wisdom for us all to share.'

Barry Manilow (below) *subscribes to the teachings of Lazaris, a disembodied spirit summoned up by Floridian channeller Jack Pursel.*

JEANE DIXON – the Celebrities' Clairvoyant

For 70 years devout Roman Catholic Jeane Dixon has predicted private and national events with outstanding accuracy.

Below: *Jeane Dixon is perhaps America's most successful and respected clairvoyant, with a career spanning many years and many influential clients.*

Jeane Dixon is one of the most remarkable clairvoyants who has ever lived, a prophet of outstanding perception and accuracy who in her lifetime has literally changed the lives of the world's most powerful people as well as the views of those who often refuted her powers. She correctly predicted the deaths of John F. Kennedy, the airplane deaths of Hollywood actress Carole Lombard and United Nations secretary-general Dag Hammarskjold, and the suicide of Marilyn Monroe. A devout Roman Catholic, she believes that her gift of second-sight comes directly from God as part of his 'divine plan' for each and every one of us.

Born Jeane Pinckert in Wisconsin in 1918, she moved to California with her parents as a toddler. As a five-year-old she said to her mother that her father would be bringing home a black and white dog that day. Her father brought a puppy home as a surprise and was baffled about how she knew about it. On another occasion she told her mother that she would shortly be receiving a 'black letter'. Two days later a black-bordered envelope announcing the death of a relative in Germany arrived through the post. It was when she was eight years old that a gypsy travelling near her home came upon her and told her mother: 'Your child is blessed with great sensitivity and wisdom.' The gypsy left the young Jeane with a crystal ball, which she went on to use as a means of concentration so that her mind became receptive to telepathic visions of future events. That gift all those years ago led to her title today of 'Seeress of Washington'. She keeps none of the money she earns from her books and lectures, preferring instead to contribute it to her non-profit-making Children to Children foundation.

As a little girl she was soon doling out advice to family and friends after gazing into her crystal ball, but it wasn't until she was married during World War 2 and living in Washington that she began crystal reading with intensity. She started doing psychic readings for servicemen at parties, but once word of her abilities began to spread she moved into a higher circle of diplomats, congressmen and other dignitaries. She was invited twice to the White House for private

consultations with President Roosevelt, but she has never revealed what she foretold for the great wartime leader.

She went on to predict major events with stunning accuracy. With the exception of 1960 she correctly foretold the outcome of each presidential election in America since 1948; she foretold the partition of India, the assassination of Mahatma Gandhi and the coming of Red China. But it was in 1963, with the murder of John F. Kennedy, that she achieved international fame. It was back in 1956 that Dixon predicted that a Democratic president 'with thick brown hair and blue eyes' would be assassinated by a man whose name began with an O or a Q. Dixon said the vision of this president's death had first come to her in 1952 when she prayed before a statue of the Virgin Mary in Washington's St Matthew's Cathedral. Dixon has always said that her premonitions came to her in three ways – by crystal gazing, by handling the treasured possession of a person or in direct messages from God. The last was the case in the prophecy of the murdered president.

It was four years until her vision was revealed to an American journalist. In 1959 she told a communist official visiting Washington from an Iron Curtain country – his name is not revealed but his identity authenticated by Dixon biographer Denis Brian – that the next president of the USA would be called Kennedy and that he would be assassinated in office. As 1963 approached, many people in the Kennedy circle were warned on numerous occasions about his impending doom, including one of

his secretaries and a secretary to his sister. Shortly before his fateful trip to Dallas, Texas, on 22 November 1963 she tried to get him to cancel his visit as the man with the name beginning with Q or O came to her in a vision. The warnings were ignored and Lee Harvey Oswald snuffed out the life of the best and brightest politician in the world with a high-powered rifle.

After his death she became known throughout the globe; her reputation was further enhanced the following year with the publication of a biography which chronicled her remarkable gifts. By 1966 she was an established international celebrity – and about to make another world-shattering prophecy.

America's manned space flight programme was within three years of putting men on the moon when Jeane suddenly had an awful premonition about the fate of the astronauts aboard an Apollo rocket. Jeane had become friendly with a woman named Jean Stout, wife of the chief of missions operations at the Office of Manned Space Flight. In December 1966 she lunched with Mrs Stout in Washington when she suddenly had a premonition that something terrible was about to happen to the Apollo programme. Holding her hand Jeane Dixon said: 'There's something strange about the floor of the capsule. It seems so thin that it almost resembles tinfoil. I am afraid that a tool dropped on it or a heel pushed firmly against it would go right through it. Under

John F. Kennedy (left). *The slaying of this president was one of many tragic premonitions of Jeane Dixon which came true.*

Below: *Carole Lombard was warned by Dixon not to take a certain plane. She ignored her – and paid for it with her life.*

Above: *The sex goddess to end them all. Her tragic death was foretold by Dixon.*

She has gone on to successfully predict the deaths of Martin Luther King, Marilyn Monroe and Robert Kennedy. When some of her prophecies have failed – like World War 3 which she forecast would break out in 1958 – she says that the basic information from God was correct and that she was merely wrong in her interpretation of the signals she received.

It is the prophecies that Mrs Dixon has written down for the end of the century that interest most observers. She predicts a great war with Russia in the Middle East and then a mighty war with China – an apocalyptic clash between good and evil which will result, by the year 2025, in China's conquest of most of Russia, Finland, Norway, Denmark, Libya and much of central Africa. On the good side, she predicts that western Europe will not feature in China's war plans and that salvation for the world will come after the war in the shape of the Second Coming of Christ.

'When that time comes,' she said, 'and it will come, we will all be united in the Brotherhood of Christ under the fatherhood of God.'

Robert Kennedy (**right**)*, the senator who shared the same fate as his brother – and whose death was also foretold by Jeane Dixon.*

the floor I see a great clump of tangled wires…I see a terrible fiery catastrophe. And it will cause the astronauts' deaths. I sense their souls leaving the blazing capsule in puffs of smoke…' On 27 January 1967 an uncontrollable blaze snuffed out the lives of three astronauts as they tested the Apollo capsule at Cape Kennedy. Electronic mal-function was cited as the cause of the disaster.

Hollywood was naturally drawn to Jeane Dixon like paperclips pulled to a magnet. She read for the Reagans – long before Ronald Reagan as president would become reliant on a seer called Joan Quigley to chart his days for him – and Bob Hope. The famous comedian once tried to test her skills by asking how many strokes he had made during a game of golf earlier that day – but he didn't mention the name of his partner on the links. Without hesitation, she replied: 'You took 92 strokes and Eisenhower took 96.' She was correct on both counts. She once told a client, actress Carole Lombard, not to travel by plane for a six-week period. Lombard chose to ignore her and died in the wreckage of her aircraft.